BRITISH COUNCIL
COLLECTION PASSPORTS

Selected by Michael Craig-Martin and Andrea Rose

British Council 2009

BRITISH COUNCIL | **75** YEARS OF CULTURAL RELATIONS

Books are to be returned on or before
the last date below.

Exhibtion
CATALOGUE

LIBREX-

Foreword
Martin Davidson

THE re-opening of the Whitechapel Gallery after two years of refurbishment and extension is a major event not only for London, but for the wider world. The innovative programming of the Whitechapel Gallery and its policy of making the best art available to as wide an audience as possible has always made it a very special place.

We are delighted to have been invited by the Whitechapel Gallery to be part of its opening celebrations and to inaugurate its Collections Gallery. Our own Collection, numbering approximately 8,500 pieces, has rarely been exhibited in the UK. For most of the 75 years of its existence, it has been overseas, doing a marvellous job forming and re-forming itself into exhibitions and displays. I am delighted that UK audiences will have the opportunity to see a significant proportion of it in the coming year.

The British Council Collection is one of the outstanding public collections of 20th- and 21st-century British art, and is seen by over a million people a year worldwide, making an important contribution to the UK's cultural relations with other countries. The works and the exhibitions they form part of are a unique reflection on the way we see ourselves and how we relate to others, bringing alive the shared culture and values of the UK for audiences overseas. In 1934, when the British Council was founded, we were charged with making connections between people to counteract a rise in nationalism across Europe and an increase in protectionism in the wake of economic hardship. Now, in our 75th Anniversary Year, I believe the need for cultural relations is as strong as ever.

I would like to thank Iwona Blazwick, Director of the Whitechapel Gallery, for proposing that our Collection should be the first to be shown in the Whitechapel's new Collections Gallery; and Andrea Tarsia, Head of Exhibitions and Projects, for working with our own staff in realising these displays: in particular, with Diana Eccles, Head of Collections, and Hannah Hunt, Exhibition Organiser.

As we celebrate our 75th Anniversary, and the Whitechapel Gallery celebrates its re-emergence as one of the capital's most forward-looking and adventurous galleries, I hope that our partnership will thrive and flourish.

Martin Davidson is Chief Executive Officer, British Council

Passports
Michael Craig-Martin

The British Council is the United Kingdom's international organisation for educational opportunities and cultural relations.

For most people the work of the British Council – what it actually does – remains obscure. This is not the case, however, for many British artists, from Henry Moore to Anya Gallaccio, who have benefited from the Council's support in helping bring their work to international recognition.

In 1978 I was pleased to be invited to make exhibitions at small galleries in Warsaw and Poznań in Poland. It is difficult now to recall the almost total isolation of the people of Eastern Europe from those in the West over many decades, and how few opportunities for cultural exchange existed.

I was able to travel to Poland to make my exhibitions and meet Polish artists and curators only because of the financial assistance of the Visual Arts Department of the British Council. I learned from my hosts that the Council also gave travel and subsistence grants to Polish artists, making it possible for them to come to London for extended periods of study and research. These exchanges, like my exhibitions, were tiny events, directly touching only handfuls of people and costing very small amounts of money, but their lasting cultural and inter-personal impact was out of all proportion, for myself as well as for my hosts.

Not all the work of the Visual Arts Department of the British Council is on such a small scale of course. Along with their other cultural and educational activities, they have organised and supported countless exhibitions of British art abroad, ranging from the modest to the blockbuster.

At the core of this work – initiated immediately following the founding of the Council in 1934 – was the gradual formation of a substantial collection of contemporary British art. Most of these artworks have rarely been seen in Britain as they have usually been on view in exhibitions overseas or hanging on the walls of British Council offices, residences and libraries around the world.

This is the first of a series of five exhibitions drawn from the British Council Collection to be shown in the new Collections Gallery at the re-opening Whitechapel. They are intended to bring the Collection to the attention of audiences here in Britain, to let them see the work that has been acquired in their name.

Invited to curate this introductory exhibition, I was daunted by the number of works in the Collection (over 8,500), particularly in view of the limitation of space available. As well as paintings and sculptures, the Collection contains photographs, installations, films and videos, watercolours, drawings, and prints.

Trying to gain an overview of the highlights of the Collection, I was shown that every work carried what is referred to as its 'passport'. These passports contain not only the usual information on the work (artist, title, date, materials) but also its purchase date and price and a complete record of its exhibition history.

Two things immediately struck me: first, how little had been paid for many of the works, and second, how remarkably extensive were their exhibition histories.

Looking across a range of dates of purchase and the prices paid, it became clear to me that the reason so many works had been purchased relatively inexpensively was because they were acquired early in the artist's career, when such a purchase might be genuinely useful to the artist and before a hyper-active market in their work had been established. The Council was not following the market, but anticipating it.

Of course, we all know that the price of the artworks, even those by young artists, has risen very substantially over the past 50 or 60 years, and not every work was bought at a notably low price. But it is clear

from the evidence that these works were purchased on the basis of expertise and conviction about their quality and importance – sophisticated and honourable collecting indeed.

It is unusual to learn the original price of a work in a public collection, and when we do it is normally because the price is considered scandalously high, not surprisingly low. It is seen as inappropriate or irrelevant, a superficial distraction from the true value of the work itself. Normally I would agree, but examining these passports, it seemed to me that what they reveal is absolute proof of the value of the proper use of public money to support the arts. I thought others would find this information as interesting as I did.

Lucian Freud's *Girl with Roses* was purchased in 1948 for £157 10s. od.; Patrick Caulfield's *View Inside a Cave* in 1969 for £500; Anish Kapoor's *The Chant of Blue* in 1983 for £3,000: Peter Doig's *Hill Houses* in 1991 for £2,700; Damien Hirst's *Apotryptophanae* in 1994 for £8,500.

I had forgotten that the first works of mine to enter the Collection were four drawings purchased in 1973 from the Rowan Gallery for £153. I must have received 50 per cent of this amount, i.e. £76.50. I can't recall how I spent the money, but I do remember being very pleased that my work had entered one of the three important public collections of contemporary art in Britain, the others being the Tate and the Arts Council.

The other revelation in the passports is the exhibition history of each work. What normally happens to a work of art after it is purchased? In general only a small number of works are shown repeatedly in exhibition after exhibition. Most disappear into private collections and live quiet lives, only occasionally disturbed, perhaps for inclusion in a retrospective. Even those in public collections spend much of their lives in storage, only occasionally seeing the light of day on exhibition or on loan.

By contrast, many works in the British Council Collection have had astonishingly extensive exhibition histories. For example, Ben Nicholson's 1935 *White Relief* has been shown in 63 exhibitions in 21 countries; Bridget Riley's 1967 *Cataract 3* in 49 exhibitions in 19 countries; Richard Deacon's 1982 *Boys and Girls (come out to play)* in 41 exhibitions in 25 countries; even Roger Hiorns' 2002 *Discipline*, purchased only in 2005, has already been shown in 8 countries.

My selection of works for this exhibition barely scratches the surface of the Collection. I have tried to give a sense of its range. For every work I felt able to include there were half a dozen I had to leave out, inevitably by artists (and friends) whose work I admire. This is a collection that contains hidden treasures, many of which I know will be included in subsequent exhibitions in this series.

Of course the world has changed dramatically over the past decades and the contemporary art world has expanded to become truly international, now integrated across every continent. The Council has an obligation to address this new world of globalised art, and if necessary to reconsider its assumptions and restructure its approach.

But in view of the current international financial crisis surely activities such as the travelling exhibitions, initiated by the Council and drawing on its existing resources, would be welcomed by cash-strapped institutions across the world? I hope that the Collection, which represents one of the most successful arms of public support for contemporary art, will continue to grow and be capitalised upon at the very moment when its potential usefulness has never been greater.

Professor Michael Craig-Martin RA CBE is Emeritus Professor of Fine Art, Goldsmiths College, University of London, and a trustee of The Art Fund.

Michael Craig-Martin
Picturing: iron, watch, safety pin, pliers, 1978

Purchased March 1979 from Rowan Gallery for £1350
Wall drawing [w]: 35mm slide and graphic tape, installation dimensions variable
Drawing [D]: plastic tape on acetate, 41.5 × 59cm
P3763

[1982] India New Delhi, Pragati Maidan, wall drawing, hereafter w [1986] Spain Madrid, Palacio de Velázquez y Palacio de Cristal, Parque del Retiro w / Spain Barcelona, Centre Cultural de la Caixa de Pensions w / Spain Museo de Bellas Artes de Bilbao w [1992] Ireland Dublin, British Council w [1994] Russia St Petersburg, State Russian Museum w [1995] Russia Moscow, New Tretyakov Gallery w / Czech Republic Prague Castle, Riding School w [1996] Morocco Casablanca, Espace Wafabank w / Germany Museum Folkwang Essen w [1997] Pakistan Karachi, Hindu Gymkhana w / Pakistan Lahore, The Old Fort w / USA Berkeley, University Art Museum, drawing, hereafter D / USA Phoenix, Arizona State University Art Museum D [1998] South Africa Johannesburg Art Gallery w / South Africa Cape Town, South African National Gallery w / Zimbabwe National Gallery Bulawayo w / Malaysia Penang Museum and Art Gallery D / Malaysia Kuala Lumpur, National Art Gallery D [1999] Zimbabwe Harare, National Gallery of Zimbabwe w / Canada Wolfville, Arcadia University Art Gallery D / Canada Timmins Museum and NEC D [2000] Cyprus Nicosia Municipal Arts Centre w / Malta Valletta, St James Cavalier Centre for Creativity w / Canada Winnipeg Art Gallery D / Canada Grande Prairie, Prairie Art Gallery D / Canada Whitehorse, Yukon Art Gallery D / Russia St Petersburg, State Hermitage Museum D [2001] Russia Moscow, Pushkin Museum of Fine Arts D / Russia Nizhny Novgorod Art Museum D / England Milton Keynes Gallery D / England Nottingham, Castle Museum and Art Gallery D / Taiwan, Taipei Fine Arts Museum w / [2004] England London, BBC w / Romania Bucharest, National Museum of Art w / [2008] Bangladesh Dhaka, Bengal Gallery of Fine Arts w Pakistan Islamabad, PNCA National Art Gallery w / Kazakhstan Almaty, State Museum of Fine Arts w [2009] Hong Kong British Council w

Monday 30th December 1974

A 17 year old boy was duck shooting on the shores of
Belfast lough. Four men approached him demanding
he hand his shotgun over. They then shot him in the
head before leaving with the weapon.

British Council Collection a brief overview
Andrea Rose

MANY of the items selected for this exhibition of works from the British Council Collection have travelled a long way to be here. Peter Doig's *Hill Houses* has come from South Africa; Chris Ofili's *Painting with Shit on it* from Nigeria; Damien Hirst's *Apotryptophanae* from Portugal; and Patrick Caulfield's *View Inside a Cave* from India. Matthew Smith's *Cornish Landscape* has been brought back from the USA; and Ben Nicholson's *1935 (White Relief)* has travelled from Spain via stops at Kendal and St Ives, where the Tate has generously allowed it to be removed from its current Nicholson exhibition specially to be shown in the Whitechapel's new Collections Gallery.

The fact that the British Council has an art collection at all is a surprise to many. Yet this is one of the greatest collections of modern and contemporary British art. Of the 3,000 or so museums and galleries listed in the *Museums & Galleries Yearbook*, only Tate Britain and the Arts Council have comparable collections of British art – that is, art that spans the past century, includes work by nearly all Britain's major artists, and encompasses painting and sculpture, drawings and watercolours, graphics, applied art, photography and, latterly, video, film and digital art.

For 75 years, the British Council has been promoting cultural relations between Britain and other countries, providing access to British thought, experience, achievement and expertise. Much of what it does in the 110 countries in which it operates is intangible, involving the exchange of people, the transfer of skills and the building of intellectual bridges – educational, scientific, academic and artistic. The Collection is quite distinct. Started in 1935, only a year after the foundation of the British Council itself, here is solid, tangible and vivid evidence of a cultural activity that has grown up alongside the Council's more usual operations, and forms a permanent, if different, aspect of its identity.

The earliest work in the Collection, which now numbers over 8,500 works, is Sickert's *St Mark's, Venice* (1896–97). This magnificent, full-frontal presentation of the façade of Venice's great church (currently included in Dulwich Picture Gallery's 'Sickert in Venice' exhibition) is a clarion call for art not to be timid or 'tasteful'. 'Taste is the death of the painter,' Sickert said. 'The more our art is serious, the more it will tend to avoid the drawing room and stick to the kitchen.'[1]

Other early works in the Collection conform to this injunction as the first stirrings of Modernism in British art are felt. Frederick Etchells' *Composition* of 1914 is a vibrant clash on paper, made when Etchells was a member of the Rebel Art Centre, a group of artists and writers keen to upset the prevailing orthodoxies. *Composition* might have been designed as the cover for the second edition of *Blast*, the magazine founded by Wyndham Lewis on the eve of the First World War as a manifesto for forward-looking art. Lewis demonstrated his principles of giving no quarter by selecting his own version of this image for the cover. His *Red Nude* (1919) entered the Collection in 1949; its red wash describing the buttocks of his sitter graphically punctuates the conventions of academic life-drawing that he so despised.

Other pre-war artists in the Collection, such as Matthew Smith, Gwen John, Spencer Gore and Harold Gilman, were influenced by innovations they saw taking shape on the Continent. Smith had studied with Matisse in Paris, and his high-keyed Cornish landscapes and voluptuous nudes – the British Council Collection holds a number of these, including the extraordinary *Fitzroy Street Nude No. 2* (1916) – owe a debt to French art. Like the Camden Town views of Gilman

Opposite: Paul Seawright, 'Monday 30th December 1974' from *Sectarian Murders*, 1991

Walter Sickert, *St Mark's, Venice*, 1896–97

Frederick Etchells, *Composition*, 1914

1. *The Art News* (12 May 1910).

William Roberts, *Folk Dance*, 1938

and Gore in the Collection, these are Anglicised Impressionism: French sourced plus an English propensity to beef things up.

The ebb and flow of influences from outside Britain is a theme that runs throughout the Collection: how with assimilation has come readjustment, a realignment of our native contours. Britain's absorption of Sickert, as with so many artists of foreign extraction throughout the 20th century, has helped keep a native tendency to insularity at bay. Sickert himself was born in Munich, to a Danish father and Anglo-Irish mother. 'No-one', he liked to declare, 'could be more English than I am.' After the Great War, though, when the first experiments with abstraction had been all but trumped by the devastation and crazed abstractions caused by tanks and artillery, several artists turned inwards to find a new sense of order and rootedness. William Roberts, a member of the Rebel Art Centre before the war, tidied the figures in his *Folk Dance* (1938) into a stolid, rhythmic pattern, a reminder of the Celtic qualities of interlacing and silhouette that have been important in British art for well over a thousand years. David Jones, whose account of serving on the Western Front (*In Parenthesis*, 1937) is a resounding poetic narrative, delves into a remote and mythic past in a watercolour such as *Curtained Outlook* (1932). The view from a window – elementally simple – is overlaid with a sense of times past, of innumerable spirits whispering as the veil-like curtain lifts in the air, and the flowers on the window-ledge bend as if to ancient sounds. In Jones, as well as in Roberts, the debt to a Celtic past – the art of the Scots, the Welsh, the Cornish and the Irish – is palpable.

Other artists, such as Stanley Spencer and L. S. Lowry, individually redefine the notion of 'Englishness' through their work. Though the British Council Collection holds none of Spencer's great nude or figure paintings, the works that we do hold show something of his conviction that Jerusalem could be built in England's green and pleasant land. In *Port Glasgow Cemetery* (1947), a place spotted while Spencer was working as an official war artist at Lithgow's Shipyard during World War II, headstones stand or lean by grave plots, the early evening light casting shadows across the carefully painted grass and bedraggled rose bushes. The lack of anything happening in this scene, combined with its scrupulous attention to detail, emphasises the blankness of death more forcibly than many a more baleful depiction of sorrow. And Lowry, a figure whom many find difficult to reconcile with the more progressive elements of contemporary art because of his supposedly formulaic figures, shows in *Industrial City* (1948), as well as in his drawing *City Scene, St John's Parade* (1929), how great his capacity is to convey with vision the hectic and sooty life of industrial Manchester. These very English masters co-exist happily in the Collection with artists such as Ben Nicholson, Paul Nash and Henry Moore, all of whom were synthesising and abstracting the bare essentials from nature throughout the 1930s so as to re-form them into compositions of extreme clarity and simplicity. The catholicity of the Collection reflects these complexities, the magnetic pull of experimentation and formal innovation from beyond these shores swinging back to that profound 'sense of place' which our history, geography and mythology exert. Possibly one of the reasons that Moore claims such a significant part in the history of 20th-century British art (as well as in the British Council Collection) is his ability to fuse the two impulses. Influenced by the African and Pre-Columbian sculpture that he saw in the British Museum in the 1920s, his carved nudes and compositions in the British Council Collection nonetheless call up the physical background of the England he was working in: the

David Jones, *Curtained Outlook*, 1932

Stanley Spencer, *Port Glasgow Cemetery*, 1947

L.S. Lowry, *Industrial City*, 1948

Eduardo Paolozzi, *Diana as an Engine I*, 1963–66 (no.13)

great shoulders of land that rise from the sea, the softly undulating downlands, the standing stones and fossilised compressions of rock that make up the ancient countryside.

In his autobiography, *Miracles of Life*, J. G. Ballard is harsh on the likes of Moore and Hepworth. 'At the time,' he writes, 'the artists most in favour with the Arts Council, the British Council and the academic critics of the day were Henry Moore, Barbara Hepworth, John Piper and Graham Sutherland, who together formed a closed fine art world largely preoccupied with formalist experiment. The light of everyday reality never shone into the aseptic whiteness of their studio-bound imaginations.'[2] This was 1956, and Ballard was a young man of 26. He had just been to see 'This is Tomorrow' at the Whitechapel Art Gallery, and it was a revelation. Here was art that wasn't studio-bound at all (or so it seemed), but brimmed with optimism about popular culture and consumer goods. Richard Hamilton had got hold of Robby the Robot (from the film *Forbidden Planet*), and included it in his installation embodying his vision of the future. Eduardo Paolozzi, the Scottish-born son of Italian immigrants, worked with the architects Peter and Alison Smithson to create a post-nuclear shelter: it consisted of an expanse of sand and the bare necessities for survival – a power drill, a bicycle wheel and a gun. Hamilton's and Paolozzi's works in the Collection retain all the excitement and fizz that they first brought to the Whitechapel in 1956. Hamilton's three vacuum-moulded 'Guggenheim prints' are shining examples of technology pressed into service to create a revolutionary idea of what a 'print' could be: here a seductive hybrid of sculpture, architecture, relief and print. Paolozzi's *Diana as an Engine I* (1963–66) is an ecstatic goddess fashioned out of engine parts and given paintwork as flawless as that of a new car. Produced at the same time as the Mini was rolling off the production lines making smart car ownership affordable for the majority of the working population for the first time, *Diana* seems a fitting deity for the 1960s. The tips of her lipstick-red arms point expansively outwards, while her submarine-yellow base stands firmly on the ground.

Within the space of the Whitechapel's new Collections Gallery it is not possible to show more than a few examples from the large holdings of British sculpture in our Collection. It is a commonplace that sculpture has been at the forefront of innovation in 20th-century British art, with Henry Moore and Barbara Hepworth seen as the forebears of successive generations of sculptors, each overturning the achievements of their predecessors, intent on constructing anew. Perhaps less noted is how the welter of ideas, and the proliferation of different materials that characterise the achievements of 20th-century British sculpture – from the sweet chestnut leaves fastened with thorns in Andy Goldsworthy's *Sweet Chestnut Leaf Horn* (1987) to the plastic bottles of Tony Cragg's *Canoe* (1982); and from the red gerberas of Anya Gallaccio's *Preserve Beauty (New York)* (2003) to the copper sulphate crystals of Roger Hiorns' *Discipline* (2002) – have gone hand in hand with the assimilation and acceptance of new ideas from outside the mainstream Western tradition. Anish Kapoor, Shirazeh Houshiary and Mona Hatoum have all enlarged the vocabulary of British sculpture, internationalising its outlook, planting on British soil traits that have taken root with exceptional vigour. As the British Council Collection circulates further and further afield, and is shown in parts of the world where the need to establish common cause is ever more critical, this cross-fertilisation is especially important. In Iran, where works from the Collection were shown in a major exhibition of 20th-century sculpture

2. J.G. Ballard, *Miracles of Life: an autobiography* (London: Fourth Estate, 2008).

Andy Goldsworthy, *Sweet Chestnut Leaf Horn*, 1987

13

3. 'Turning Points', shown at Tehran Museum of Contemporary Art, Iran, March–May 2004. Artists included: Anthony Caro, Tony Cragg, Richard Deacon, Barry Flanagan, Anya Gallaccio, Gilbert & George, Mona Hatoum, Barbara Hepworth, Damien Hirst, Shirazeh Houshiary, Anish Kapoor, Richard Long, Henry Moore, Eduardo Paolozzi and Bill Woodrow.

in 2004, Kapoor's *The Chant of Blue* (1983), took on new colorations as its domed shapes and deep blue surfaces seemed to reflect the blue-tiled mosques of Isfahan, and black shapes cast on the street by women wearing chadors.[3] And Houshiary's *Gravity* (2004), a pulsating circle radiating from the tightly-wound centre of the canvas, seemed an appropriate image from a London-based artist, born in Shiraz, to send back to her native Iran: exhalation and exhilaration caught in a spiral of meanings.

In this first exhibition from the British Council's Collection at the Whitechapel Gallery, however, painting takes the lion's share of space. In part this is due to space restrictions, in part because the Collection has grown pragmatically during the past 75 years; paintings – or flat works – have by and large been easier to transport overseas than sculpture, the idealism of the British Council (founded initially to combat the forces of Fascism and now to build trust across the globe) being underpinned by practicality. But painting in Britain is as remarkable, I would argue, as sculpture. No painters produce work without a nod in the direction of their predecessors, and in many cases a sort of squaring up to them. In the case of British art, this is usually directed at the tradition of European classical painting, pronounced dead many years ago, but revived and reinstated with enormous determination by generations of British painters since the end of World War II. Even at the height of the Pop Art movement in the early 1960s, when his peers were looking towards America, Patrick Caulfield was re-examining the worn-out conventions of European painting – the still life, the 'view', the interior. In *The Blue Posts* (1989), he gets to grips with the central concerns of European art within a pub interior – how light affects the look of things, how to organise space, how to reconcile the many different ways of looking, from the photo-realistic half-pint of lager to the sliver of pink wallpaper thrown up by a chink of light from an unseen window. For an older generation of British painters, European painting has also been at the heart of a very English revolution. The group of artists loosely associated as the 'School of London' – among them Francis Bacon, Lucian Freud, Frank Auerbach, Leon Kossoff, Euan Uglow and R. B. Kitaj – has concentrated almost exclusively on painting people and places they know. Like Sickert, several were not born in Britain. Like Sickert, they have brought urgency and compulsion to British art, with a healthy disdain for decorativeness and 'good taste'. Francis Bacon, regrettably not represented in the British Council Collection, was the first to demonstrate, in the late 1940s, that the figure could be prime material for painting once more, even if it was only a blind, dismembered thing howling with rage. In the hands of Freud, Auerbach and Kossoff, there has been an undeviating focus on painting from observation. This has produced some of the most intensely felt and enduring works in British art: from Freud's *Girl with Roses* (1947–48) to Auerbach's *Head of J.Y.M. III* (1980) and Kossoff's small fireball of a painting, *View of Dalston Junction* (1974).

The selection of works for this first exhibition from the British Council Collection at the Whitechapel Gallery has been made by Michael Craig-Martin, and we are enormously grateful to him for undertaking this. Craig-Martin has refined his choices by focusing on 'great early buys': works that have been purchased early in an artist's career, and for relatively modest sums (the small acquisition budget available for the Collection being happily allied to the virtue of 'a good eye'). Together with the prices paid at the time for these works, we are also publishing here their 'passport' details, showing not only how

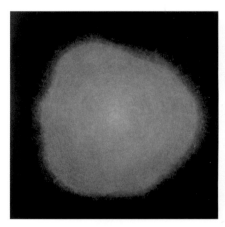

Shirazeh Houshiary, *Gravity*, 2004

Patrick Caulfield, *The Blue Posts*, 1989

Frank Auerbach, *Head of J.Y.M. III*, 1980

Bill Brandt, *Ironworks, Sheffield*, 1937

Keith Arnatt, from the *Liverpool Beach Burial* series, 1968

prescient successive purchasers have been, but how well the works have been utilised once they have joined the British Council Collection. Dates and countries in which works have been shown appear alongside the corresponding text and image, but at the back of the catalogue individual exhibition titles can be found under 'Exhibition Histories'. Some works will be on show in the exhibition but do not appear as full-page entries in the catalogue: among them Paul Seawright's c-type colour print 'Monday 30th December 1974', from his series entitled *Sectarian Murders* (1989); Bill Brandt's photograph of the ironworks in Sheffield, one of 60 vintage photographs by Brandt in the Collection; Tim Head's *Toxic Lagoon* (1987), *Deluge* (1985) and *Fall Out* (1985), which stand in for Head's *Still Life* (1978) since we are unable here to show the complete installation. There are other works that Craig-Martin would have liked to include but which are committed to exhibitions elsewhere; these include Keith Arnatt's three photographs from the *Liverpool Beach Burial* series (1968), fine examples of some of the first conceptual works to be made using photography, but now on loan to the Henry Moore Institute, Leeds, for their exhibition 'Box, Body, Burial: the sculptural imagination of Keith Arnatt'. These choices hint at some of the depth and richness of the Collection, but can only hint at it. Over the coming year, other curators will follow with selections of their own: Jeremy Deller and Alan Kane, compilers of the *Folk Archive*, a compendium of a certain type of 'Britishness'; Nicholas Penny, Director of the National Gallery; and finally the Portuguese-born painter Paula Rego. They will no doubt bring out a telling variety of different works, and the Collection will appear in new incarnations during every exhibition. To all of them we extend our warmest thanks.

This series of exhibitions at the Whitechapel is a rare opportunity for the British Council to show some of its Collection in Britain. For most of its life, much of the Collection (approximately 60 per cent at any one time) is on exhibition or display overseas, to inspire and enthuse international audiences, first and foremost with British art and, by extension, with the broader culture from which it emanates. For many years the Council has organised its own programme of exhibitions drawn from the holdings of the Collection. These have been primarily for parts of the world where local circumstances make it difficult for organisers to mount exhibitions of original works of art.[4] At the time of writing, for instance, a new exhibition drawn from recent film and video work in the Collection is opening in Damascus, to be shown right across the old city using places and spaces that have never entertained contemporary art before.[5] Until relatively recently, some twenty such exhibitions a year were in international circulation, some of them in far-away parts of the world to which lenders would be reluctant to see their works sent for long and often arduous tours. For example, we have until recently been working to establish a network of twelve museums and galleries across Russia, all of them outside Moscow and St Petersburg. Six of these were in Siberia, six west of the Urals. Few of these museums, many of them grand Beaux-Arts-style institutions, have had much contact with art from outside Russia before, and each has selected groups of works from our Collection, providing them with an opening on the Western world. This programme necessarily entails journeys of huge distances, to places that few British artworks have travelled before, and with loans that could be on the road for years at a time. This sounds potentially hazardous, but all works are carefully assessed for travel before they set out, and only certain works travel to certain places. That said, the Collection exists to travel adventurously, in the belief that a connected world is

4. Exhibitions from the Collection were toured extensively in the developing world throughout the 1960s to 1990s. Rungwe Kingdon, who grew up in Kampala during the 1960s, and who today is building a sculpture foundry in western Uganda as a resource for artists from across East Africa, has commented on what it was like to be on the receiving end of these exhibitions: 'Growing up in East Africa in the 1960s, some of the first art I became aware of was from the British Council's touring exhibitions, the product of people of vision and expertise creating meaningful cultural ties between Britain and other countries, not only in Africa but all over the world. The impact these exhibitions and catalogues had, not just on me, but on thousands of other people, was enormous; the sponsorship and scholarships for individuals and projects an incalculable advantage enjoyed mutually in Britain and abroad.' Published in *Arts Industry* (11 January 2008).

5. 'Flicker': an exhibition of recent British film and video to be shown across the old city of Damascus. Artists include: Haluk Akakçe, Tacita Dean, Willie Doherty, Susan Hiller, Rachel Lowe, Christina Mackie, Rosalind Nashashibi, Thomson & Craighead, and Wood & Harrison.

6. Full details of all the exhibitions organised by Visual Arts Department are available online at http://collection.britishcouncil.org . The records of the Department's Advisory Committee Meetings are also available to view on request. These provide a detailed history of the work of Visual Arts Department, and include reports and minutes of all the Department's business, from 1935 to 2007. The Visual Arts Advisory Committee was disbanded in 2007.

better than an unconnected one; and that relationships inevitably involve risk and exposure.

No collection of this size and scope could have been assembled without the goodwill and generosity of the artists themselves. Funding for the Collection has always been slender, and its growth has largely been due to the close working relationship between Britain's artists and the British Council's Visual Arts Department, a relationship that has developed out of the huge international exhibition programme organised by the Council over seven decades, with catalogues published by the Department and full education programmes to support these.[6] Until recently, around sixty exhibitions annually were being supported by the Council through its Visual Arts programme, some from the Collection as noted above, but the majority of them exhibitions of borrowed material that might tour to as many as three venues, and then be returned to lenders. These exhibitions have been fertile ground for the Collection, providing us with insights, information, privileged access, knowledge and, most importantly, a day-to-day relationship with the artists with whom we have worked, so that the Collection has grown as a branch grows out of a tree.

The invitation to show our Collection at the newly extended Whitechapel Gallery provides an opportunity to examine the record of the Collection, and to take stock. The themes that emerge from the texts written by all five of the writers commissioned for this catalogue suggest a running tension between the pursuit of modernity on the one hand, and a native specificity on the other – between the competing pressures of globalisation and cultural identity, if you will. These are themes with which the British Council is concerned at all levels and in all areas of its work: how societies balance the claims of the past with those of the future; how certain regions of the world can 'modernise' without 'westernising'; and how art and education can contribute to building trust between people without threatening to destabilise the existing order. As the British Council reviews its work in the light of changing international circumstances, the work of the Collection, too, comes under the spotlight. Inevitably, in an era of global e-communications, we need to ask whether it is still valuable to tour real works of art internationally. Or whether the word 'British' is still a worthwhile prefix to attach to the word 'art', particularly when as Europeans we might be thinking of a more federated approach. Is the expertise that comes with the Collection being capitalised upon to the maximum, and might it be offered not only internationally but within Britain, too? And can we take as an affirmation of the power of art to move and resonate, the comment about Richard Long's *Stone Line* (1979) made to me by the President of Bulgaria when I showed him round an exhibition in Sofia, shortly

Richard Long, *Stone Line*, 1979 (no.23)

after the dismantling of the Iron Curtain? 'Ah,' he said, looking at the twenty-three bars of Cornish slate lined up on the floor, 'you know, this is exactly how I feel as President.' Such questions are bound to be asked in relation to a collection with our name and our history. I suggest that the works of art themselves provide both answer and argument.

Andrea Rose is Director of Visual Arts, British Council

CATALOGUE

Sizes are given in centimetres, height followed by width followed by depth (in the case of sculpture or multi-media works).

Numbers prefixed by the letter P are the British Council Collection accession numbers.

In the 'passport' details accompanying each individual work, we have given names of countries and cities as they were at the time when our works were shown there. We have not revised place names to reflect today's political boundaries. We are also providing the details of the price paid by the British Council for each work in the currency of the day: thus pounds (£), shillings (s.) and pence (d.) prior to decimalisation in 1971. Again, we are not revising these prices to reflect current valuations. Titles and dates of exhibitions are listed separately under 'Exhibition Histories' at the back of this publication.

We have made every effort to make tour details as comprehensive as possible, but in those cases indicated with an asterisk*, we have been unable to confirm either exact venues, or indeed all the countries these exhibitions visited.

The authors of the catalogue texts are indicated by their initials:

DF Dorothy Feaver
JL Jessica Lack
AL Alex Leicester
LMF Laura McLean-Ferris
RP Richard Parry

Purchased August 1946
from The Redfern Gallery
for £132 6s. od.
Oil on canvas, 49.5 × 73.2cm
P3

PAUL Nash was recuperating from a nasty bout of bronchitis in the summer of 1933 when he first came across the Avebury megaliths, the largest prehistoric stone circle in Europe. He recalled, 'Some were half covered by the grass, others stood up in cornfields were entangled and overgrown in the copses, some were buried under the turf. But they were wonderful and disquieting, and, as I saw them then, I shall always remember them.'[1] Appropriately, and as was often the case, Nash painted *Landscape of the Megaliths* from memory (convalescence had taken him to the Riviera); the stones are a nexus for the entanglement of the past in present-day landscape.

This is a quietly 'disquieting' image. Andrew Causey has criticised it as 'not so much abstract as empty', yet the idea of emptiness is crucial.[2] This is a pre-industrial, uninhabited vista, replete with uncanny repetitions; the hilltop copses to left and right look towards Nash's late oils of Wittenham woods, another prehistoric site. It is dominated by the outlines of two stones, ensnaring a range of fragmentary associations, to disorientating effect. The larger outline has a druidic circle inscribed in a central position, around which swirl hilltops, clouds and shadows, the near and distant united in orbit. There is a grandeur to the sweeping connection made between the contemporary landscape and the ancient past, matched by Nash's mysterious aerial perspective, which nods to the pioneering use of aerial archaeology adopted by Alexander Keiller, who bought the Avebury site in 1924 to protect it from the threat of a Marconi wireless station.

The development of hands-off archaeology is paralleled by the painting's unobtrusive surface and even, un-muddy planes of colour. There are dashes of lichen-like texture within the outlined stones, but above all the avoidance of prominent physical textures draws attention to the picture's peculiar decomposition of space, serving to distance us from the physicality of the landscape, and instead reduce its atmosphere – the *genius loci* – to a pure consommé. In a letter (14 April 1934) to his first biographer, Anthony Bertram, Nash insisted that although he wasn't abandoning painting after Nature, 'I want a wider aspect, a different angle of vision as it were.'[3]

Landscape of the Megaliths was first exhibited under the title *Landscape Composition*, in Unit One's only exhibition, and it tries to reconcile the 'battle lines' that Nash, the group's driving force, detected between going Modern and being British: 'internationalism versus the pastoral; the functional versus the futile.'[4] Indeed, the decision to rename the painting to its present, relational title draws attention to Nash's fascination with what he called the 'mystery of relationship' – something that was imminently to attract him to Surrealism. Those conceptual battles lines, however, were as much the legacy of Nash's experiences as an official war artist on the Western Front. Nash was to make a peculiarly English translation of Surrealism, from the perspective of – as he called himself – a 'war artist without a war'. So too, *Landscape of the Megaliths* rethinks the famous lines of Rupert Brooke's already classic poem, 'The Soldier' (1914):

> If I should die, think only this of me:
> That there's some corner of a foreign field
> That is forever England. ...

Landscape of the Megaliths is a vision of the foreign-ness of English fields; it is a vision filtered through the archaeologist's windscreen, or the binoculars of a new breed of English tourist, motoring out into rural parts armed with Shell guides and ordnance survey maps.   DF

1. Paul Nash, 'Picture History', notes on work 1933–45 prepared for his dealers, Albert Tooth and Sons (1943–45), quoted in Andrew Causey, *Paul Nash* (Oxford: Clarendon Press, 1980), 246.

2. Causey (1980), 257.

3. Nash quoted in *Paul Nash: Paintings and Watercolours*, exh. cat. (London: Tate Gallery, 1975), 83–84.

4. Paul Nash, 'Going Modern and Being British', *Weekend Review* (12 March 1932).

Purchased March 1948
from the artist for £120 0s. od.
Oil on carved and built up wood,
54.5 × 80cm
P31

It is, you might say, simply a lavatory artform, a clean antiseptic bath-room art which extracts from their functions the splash-board and the lavatory basin and sets them sleeping and dreaming together in a world whose objects are forbidden to have associations.
Gordon Porteus, 1935[1]

THE words of critic Gordon Porteus, writing in *New English Weekly* in 1935, sum up with aplomb something of the battle between the new forms of Modern Art that was raging across the Channel. For Porteus, Nicholson was headed towards the 'abyss of the absolute' and an outlook disinfected of human trace.[2] Nicholson was a prominent member of Unit One, a group of painters, sculptors and architects initially headed by Paul Nash. Nash discerned that there were two streams of thinking for the contemporary artist: the 'pursuit of form' and the 'pursuit of the soul'.[3] This delineation captures something of the divide that existed between artists such as Nicholson who sought the 'Constructive', and those of a Surrealist persuasion. It is possible to see this division in terms of an Apollonian and Dionysian opposition seeth-ing within the orbit of Hampstead, where many of these artists lived.

Another contemporary concern that Porteus's words highlight is that of the possibilities of health and societal nourishment within the new Modern architecture. Around this time, many of the leading pioneers of Modern architecture, including Erich Mendelsohn, Berthold Lubetkin and later Walter Gropius, were coming to Britain, seeking refuge from totalitarian developments abroad. Their buildings, including Lubetkin's Finsbury Health Centre (1938), sought to promote the nourishing social qualities of clean white spaces and plenty of natural light and air, at a time when urban living for a significant part of the working population consisted of slum-based deprivation. The Constructive artists similarly sought to create forms that were imbued with the same spirit of utopian purity through abstraction.

In this light, the 'White Reliefs' (all produced between 1934 and 1937) were Nicholson's zenith. They represented a move away from canvas to board, and from subject to object, where the object becomes the embodiment of an idea of perfection. Each one is a *tabula rasa*, a microcosm of the infinite, which 'should be seen as something like a new world', as Nash put it.[4] The white has a purity and a metaphysical dimension, beyond place and temporality, a sense of the pregnant void that owes a debt to Malevich. On one level, this gesture might seem out of touch with the realities that were bearing down on world events, given the economic depression, national rearmament and the rise of Fascism in Europe. And yet it is possible to see these works as icons of hope and clarity: moments of a glimpsed cohesion, hermetically sealed within a frame, set against the general confusion of the era. Nicholson himself explained, 'As I see it, painting and religious experience are the same thing, and what we are all searching for is the understanding and realisation of infinity – an ideal which is complete, with no beginning, no end and therefore giving to all things for all time.'[5]   R P

1. Porteus quoted in Jeremy Lewison, *Ben Nicholson: The Years of Experiment 1919–39*, exh. cat. (Cambridge: Kettle's Yard Gallery, 1983), 28.

2. Ibid., 33.

3. Nash quoted in Lewison, 24.

4. Ibid., 33.

5. Nicholson quoted in Lewison, 33.

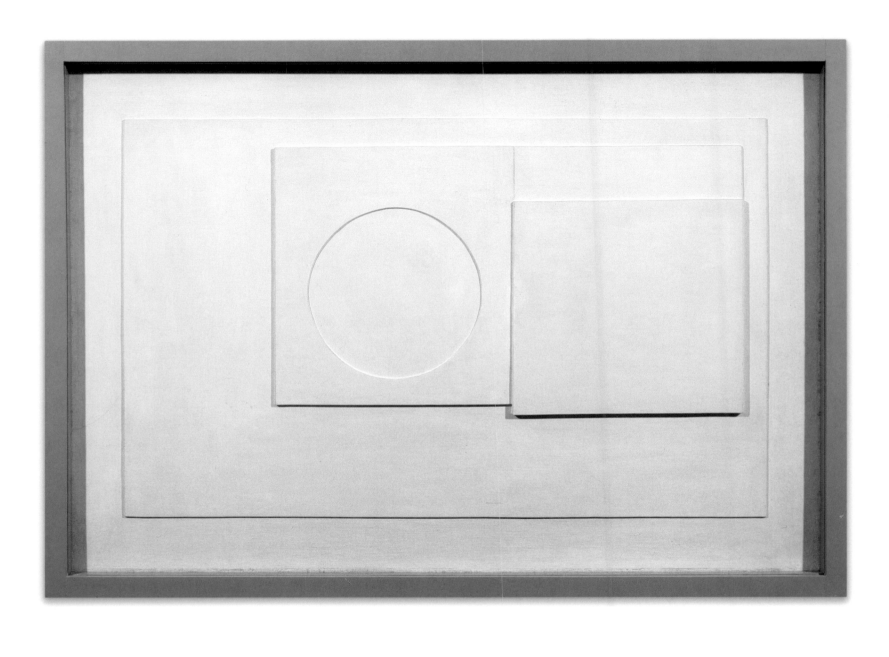

Three sculptures by Henry Moore

FOR many years Henry Moore's bronze sculpture *Large Spindle Piece* (1974) sat on a plinth outside the British Council's head-quarters on The Mall in London, just one among his legacy of public monuments across the world. Moore's sculptures were born out of two world wars and the glories of the machine age, and from Scotland to Saudi Arabia, his bronze and slate-coloured hulks brood over the landscape like monoliths from an earlier era, presiding over global disasters with a prophetic power. Yet their rugged textures and simple forms were equally inspired by the Yorkshire countryside of his childhood, and the sculptures featured in this exhibition belong, specifically, to the period when Moore was living in Hampstead with his wife, Irina Radetsky.

The North London suburb was then a playground of the bohemian set, and a particular group of artists had settled there, including Barbara Hepworth, Ben Nicholson and Naum Gabo, all of whom had an influence on the young Moore's move towards abstraction. Moore's early sculpture was informed by his interest in non-Western art – particularly Pre-Columbian art – and in direct carving in wood and stone. He recognised that he could reinvent the way we see human figures as a result: bold, abstract, full of expressive force despite the fact – or because of it – that it did not conform to the canons of perspective and proportion that had governed Western classical sculpture since the Greeks and Romans. Previously regarded in Britain solely as objects of archaeological or ethnographic interest, these non-Western sculptures encouraged the simple monumentality of Moore's early carvings, as well as their emphasis on their material qualities – their 'stoniness' and a sense of mass. *Girl with Clasped Hands*, carved from Cumberland alabaster the year after his marriage, and *Composition*, made a few years later from polished concrete over an iron armature, exemplify this, infused with the warmth of Moore's personality. 'I am very much aware that associational, psychological factors play a large part in sculpture,' he wrote in an article for *The Listener* (18 August 1937). 'I think the humanist, organic element will always be for me of fundamental importance in sculpture, giving sculpture its vitality.' While Moore admired Epstein's and Brancusi's insistence on direct carving and truth to materials, *Composition* appears intent on stretching beyond the capabilities of its rigid medium. Its wriggling cavities are suggestive of a human form struggling to break free.

In 1936, Moore signed the Surrealist Manifesto and, having visited Spain just two years before, was very much affected by the outbreak of the Spanish Civil War. He petitioned Parliament on their non-intervention and attempted to travel to Spain as one of a delegation of artists and writers that included Auden and Spender; but he was refused a travel permit by the British government. From this time, *Mother and Child* is a strange, amorphous form in which two figures appear to be melting into, or emerging out of, one another, the stone as soft as if a hand had squeezed it into shape. The work continues to embody Moore's conflict between the forces of Surrealism and abstraction, but it has a new emotional charge. Caught in its own materiality, it remains a sensitive record of the predicament of mankind, caught, incessantly, in its own crossfire.   AL

Opposite: detail from Henry Moore, *Composition*, 1933 (no.5)

Purchased March 1948
from E. Brown and Phillips
for £250 0s. 0d.
Cumberland alabaster,
height 38.1cm

P25

[**1948**] **Italy** Venice Biennale / **Italy** Milan, Galleria d'Arte Moderna [**1949**] **England** Wakefield Art Gallery / **England** Manchester City Art Gallery [**1949–51**] **Belgium** Brussels, Palais des Beaux-Arts / **France** Paris, Musée National d'Art Moderne / **Netherlands** Stedelijk Museum Amsterdam / **Federal Republic of Germany** Kunstverein in Hamburg / **Federal Republic of Germany** Düsseldorf, Kunstverein für die Rheinlande und Westfalen / **Switzerland** Kunsthalle Bern / **Greece** Athens, Zappeion Gallery [**1951**] **England** London, Tate Gallery [**1952**] **South Africa** Cape Town, South African National Gallery / **Sweden** Stockholm, Akademien / **Sweden** Norrköping, Akademien / **Sweden** Örebro, Akademien / **Sweden** Göteborgs Konstmuseum, Konsthall [**1953**] **Denmark** Copenhagen, Kunstforeningen / **Norway** Oslo, Kunstnernes Hus / **Norway** Trondhjiems Kunstforening / **Norway** Bergen Kunstforening / **Netherlands** Rotterdam, Museum Boijmans Van Beuningen / **Brazil** São Paulo Bienal [**1955**] **Yugoslavia** Skopje, Daud Pash Hamaki / **Yugoslavia** Belgrade, Kalemegdan Pavilion / **Switzerland** Kunsthalle Basel / **Yugoslavia** Zagreb, Tomislav Pavilion / **Yugoslavia** Ljubljana, Moderna Galerija / **Canada** Musée des Beaux-Arts de Montréal / **Canada** Ottawa, National Gallery of Canada [**1956**] **Canada** Toronto, Art Gallery of Ontario / **Canada** Winnipeg Art Gallery / **Canada** Vancouver Art Gallery / **New Zealand** Auckland, City Art Gallery / **New Zealand** Christchurch, Robert McDougall Art Gallery [**1957**] **New Zealand** Dunedin Public Art Gallery / **New Zealand** Wellington, National Art Gallery / **South Africa** Port Elizabeth, King George VI Art Gallery / **Rhodesia** Salisbury, Rhodes Centenary Museum and Art Gallery / **Rhodesia** Bulawayo, National Museum / **South Africa** Johannesburg Art Gallery [**1959**] **Portugal** Lisbon, Palácio Foz / **Portugal** Porto, School of Fine Arts / **Spain** Madrid, National Library / **Spain** Barcelona, Hospital of Santa Cruz / **Poland** Warsaw, Zachęta Gallery / **Poland** Kraków, Society of Fine Arts / **Poland** Poznań, Muzeum Narodowe [**1960**] **Poland** Wrocław, Zachęta Gallery / **Poland** Szczecin, Muzeum Narodowe / **Federal Republic of Germany** Hamburger Kunsthalle / **Federal Republic of Germany** Museum Folkwang Essen / **Switzerland** Kunsthaus Zürich / **Federal Republic of Germany** Munich, Haus der Kunst / **Italy** Rome, Galleria Nazionale d'Arte Moderna [**1961**] **France** Paris, Musée Rodin / **Netherlands** Stedelijk Museum Amsterdam / **Federal Republic of Germany** Berlin, Akademie der Künste / **Austria** Vienna, Akademie der Bildenden Künste / **Denmark** Humlebaek, Louisiana Museum of Modern Art [**1963**] **England** Wakefield Art Gallery / **England** Hull,

Ferens Art Gallery [**1964**] **Mexico** Mexico City, Museo de Arte Moderno / **Brazil** Museu de Arte Moderna do Rio de Janeiro / **Venezuela** Museo de Bellas Artes de Caracas [**1965**] **Argentina** Buenos Aires, Museo Nacional de Bellas Artes [**1966**] **Romania** Bucharest, Sala Dalles / **Czechoslovakia** Bratislava, Slovak National Gallery / **Czechoslovakia** Prague, Národní Galerie / **Israel** Jerusalem, Israel Museum / **Israel** Tel Aviv Museum of Art [**1967**] **Hungary** Budapest, Műcsarnok [**1969**] **Japan** Tokyo, National Museum of Modern Art / **Japan** Osaka, Hanshin Department Store / **Japan** Nagoya, Meitetsu Department Store [**1970**] **Hong Kong** Museum of Art [**1972**] **Italy** Florence, Forte di Belvedere [**1973**] **Luxembourg** Musée d'État [**1977**] **France** Paris, Musée de l'Orangerie des Tuileries [**1981–82**] **Spain** Madrid, Palacio de Velázquez y Palacio de Cristal, Parque del Retiro / **Portugal** Lisbon, Fundação Calouste Gulbenkian / **Spain** Barcelona, Fundació Joan Miró [**1982**] **Mexico** Mexico City, Museo de Arte Moderno [**1983**] **Venezuela** Museo de Bellas Artes de Caracas [**1986**] **Hong Kong** Museum of Art and Visual Arts Centre / **Japan** Tokyo, Metropolitan Art Gallery / **Japan** Fukuoka Art Museum [**1987**] **India** New Delhi, National Gallery of Modern Art [**1988**] **England** London, Royal Academy of Arts [**1990**] **USSR** Kiev, Ukrainian Museum of Fine Art [**1991**] **Luxembourg** Musée National d'Histoire et d'Art / **Bulgaria** Sofia, Cyril Methodius Foundation / **Argentina** Buenos Aires, Museo Nacional de Bellas Artes [**1992**] **Australia** Sydney, Art Gallery of New South Wales [**1993**] **Hungary** Budapest, Museum of Fine Arts / **Slovakia** Bratislava, Mirbach Palace and Palffy Palace / **Czech Republic** Prague, Central Bohemian Gallery–Carolinum [**1995**] **Poland** Kraków, BWA Gallery / **Poland** Warsaw, Centre for Contemporary Art / **Italy** Venice, Fondazione Giorgio Cini [**1996**] **France** Nantes, Musée des Beaux-Arts / **Germany** Kunsthalle Mannheim [**1997**] **Cuba** Havana, Centro de Arte Contemporáneo Wifredo Lam / **Colombia** Bogotá, Museo Nacional de Colombia / **Argentina** Buenos Aires, Museo Nacional de Bellas Artes / **Uruguay** Montevideo, Museo Nacional de Artes Visuales / **Chile** Santiago, Museo Nacional de Bellas Artes [**1998**] **England** Cambridge, Kettle's Yard / **England** Bexhill-on-Sea, De La Warr Pavilion / **England** Norwich, Sainsbury Centre for Visual Arts [**1999**] **Germany** Cologne, Wallraf-Richartz-Museum [**2000**] **China** Beijing, China Art Gallery / **China** Guangzhou, Guangdong Museum of Art [**2001**] **China** Shanghai Art Museum / **France** Vez, Donjon de Vez [**2002**] **Germany** Kunstmuseum Wolfsburg [**2003**] **France** Toulouse, Les Abattoirs / **Germany** Frankfurt, Städelsches Kunstinstitut [**2004**] **Greece** Athens, National Gallery / **Romania** Bucharest, National Museum of Art [**2005**] **Brazil** Pinacoteca de Estado de São Paulo / **Mexico** Mexico City, Museo Dolores Olmedo Patiño / **Brazil** Rio de Janeiro, Paço Imperial / **Brazil** Brasilia, Centro Cultural Banco do Brasil [**2006**] **Spain** Caixa Forum Barcelona

Henry Moore Composition, 1933

Purchased March 1948
from the artist for £300 0s. 0d.
Concrete, height 58.4cm

P49

[1948] Italy Venice Biennale / Italy Milan, Galleria d'Arte Moderna [1949] England Wakefield Art Gallery / England Manchester City Art Gallery [1949–51] Belgium Brussels, Palais des Beaux-Arts / France Paris, Musée National d'Art Moderne / Netherlands Stedelijk Museum Amsterdam / Federal Republic of Germany Kunstverein in Hamburg / Federal Republic of Germany Düsseldorf, Kunstverein für die Rheinlande und Westfalen / Switzerland Kunsthalle Bern / Greece Athens, Zappeion Gallery [1951] England London, Tate Gallery [1952] South Africa Cape Town, South African National Gallery / Sweden Stockholm, Akademien / Sweden Norrköping, Akademien / Sweden Örebro, Akademien / Sweden Göteborgs Konstmuseum, Konsthall [1953] Denmark Copenhagen, Kunstforeningen / Norway Oslo, Kunstnernes Hus / Norway Trondhjiems Kunstforening / Norway Bergen Kunstforening / Netherlands Rotterdam, Museum Boijmans Van Beuningen / Brazil São Paulo Bienal [1955] Yugoslavia Skopje, Daud Pash Hamaki / Yugoslavia Belgrade, Kalemegdan Pavilion / Switzerland Kunsthalle Basel / Yugoslavia Zagreb, Tomislav Pavilion / Yugoslavia Ljubljana, Moderna Galerija / Canada Musée des Beaux-Arts de Montréal / Canada Ottawa, National Gallery of Canada [1956] Canada Toronto, Art Gallery of Ontario / Canada Winnipeg Art Gallery / Canada Vancouver Art Gallery / New Zealand Auckland, City Art Gallery / New Zealand Christchurch, Robert McDougall Art Gallery [1957] New Zealand Dunedin Public Art Gallery / New Zealand Wellington, National Art Gallery / South Africa Port Elizabeth, King George VI Art Gallery / Rhodesia Salisbury, Rhodes Centenary Museum and Art Gallery / Rhodesia Bulawayo, National Museum / South Africa Johannesburg Art Gallery [1959] Portugal Lisbon, Palácio Foz / Portugal Porto, School of Fine Arts / Spain Madrid, National Library / Spain Barcelona, Hospital of Santa Cruz / Poland Warsaw, Zachęta Gallery / Poland Kraków, Society of Fine Arts / Poland Poznań, Muzeum Narodowe [1960] Poland Wrocław, Zachęta Gallery / Poland Szczecin, Muzeum Narodowe / Federal Republic of Germany Hamburger Kunsthalle / Federal Republic of Germany Museum Folkwang Essen / Switzerland Kunsthaus Zürich / Federal Republic of Germany Munich, Haus der Kunst / Italy Rome, Galleria Nazionale d'Arte Moderna [1961] France Paris, Musée Rodin / Netherlands Stedelijk Museum Amsterdam / Federal Republic of Germany Berlin, Akademie der Künste / Austria Vienna, Akademie der Bildenden Künste / Denmark Humlebaek, Louisiana Museum of Modern Art [1962] England Leeds City Art Gallery [1966] Romania Bucharest, Sala Dalles / Czechoslovakia Bratislava, Slovak National Gallery / Czechoslovakia Prague, Národní Galerie / Israel Jerusalem, Israel Museum / Israel Tel Aviv Museum of Art [1967] Ireland Dublin, Trinity College [1968] Netherlands Otterlo, Rijksmuseum Kröller-Müller / Federal Republic of Germany Kunsthalle Düsseldorf / Netherlands Rotterdam, Museum Boijmans Van Beuningen [1969] Federal Republic of Germany Staatliche Kunsthalle Baden-Baden / Federal Republic of Germany Kunsthalle Bielefeld / Federal Republic of Germany Darmstadt, Institut Mathildenhöhe / Federal Republic of Germany Nuremberg, Städtische Kunstsammlung [1972] Italy Florence, Forte di Belvedere [1973] Luxembourg Musée d'État [1974] Scotland Edinburgh, Scottish Arts Council [1977] France Paris, L'Orangerie des Tuileries [1978] England Portsmouth City Art Gallery [1981–82] Spain Madrid, Palacio de Velázquez y Palacio de Cristal, Parque del Retiro / Portugal Lisbon, Fundação Calouste Gulbenkian / Spain Barcelona, Fundació Joan Miró [1982] England Durham, DLI Museum and Arts Centre / England Leeds City Art Gallery [1986] Hong Kong Museum of Art and Visual Arts Centre / Japan Tokyo, Metropolitan Art Gallery / Japan Fukuoka Art Museum [1987] India New Delhi, National Gallery of Modern Art [1990] USSR Kiev, Ukrainian Museum of Fine Art [1991] Luxembourg Musée National d'Histoire et d'Art / Bulgaria Sofia, Cyril Methodius Foundation / Argentina Buenos Aires, Museo Nacional de Bellas Artes [1992] England London, British Council [2000] England Much Hadham, Henry Moore Foundation [2004] England London, Dulwich Picture Gallery / Romania Bucharest, National Museum of Art [2006] Spain Caixa Forum Barcelona [2007] Russia Moscow, State Tretyakov Gallery

Henry Moore Mother and Child, 1936

Purchased March 1948
from the artist for £300 0s. 0d.
Ancaster stone, height 51cm
P48

[1948] Italy Venice Biennale / Italy Milan, Galleria d'Arte Moderna [1949] England Wakefield Art Gallery / England Manchester City Art Gallery [1949–51] Belgium Brussels, Palais des Beaux-Arts / France Paris, Musée National d'Art Moderne / Netherlands Stedelijk Museum Amsterdam / Federal Republic of Germany Kunstverein in Hamburg / Federal Republic of Germany Düsseldorf, Kunstverein für die Rheinlande und Westfalen / Switzerland Kunsthalle Bern / Greece Athens, Zappeion Gallery [1951] England London, Tate Gallery [1952] South Africa Cape Town, South African National Gallery / Austria Vienna, Albertina [1953] Brazil São Paulo Bienal [1954–55] Switzerland Kunsthalle Basel / Yugoslavia Skopje, Daud Pash Hamaki / Yugoslavia Belgrade, Kalemegdan Pavilion / Yugoslavia Zagreb, Tomislav Pavilion / Yugoslavia Ljubljana, Moderna Galerija / Canada Musée des Beaux-Arts de Montréal / Canada Ottawa, National Gallery of Canada [1956] Canada Toronto, Art Gallery of Ontario / Canada Winnipeg Art Gallery / Canada Vancouver Art Gallery / New Zealand Auckland, City Art Gallery / New Zealand Christchurch, Robert McDougall Art Gallery [1957] New Zealand Dunedin Public Art Gallery / South Africa Port Elizabeth, King George VI Art Gallery / Rhodesia Salisbury, Rhodes Centenary Museum and Art Gallery / Rhodesia Bulawayo, National Museum / South Africa Johannesburg Art Gallery [1959] Portugal Lisbon, Palácio Foz / Portugal Porto, School of Fine Arts / Spain Madrid, National Library / Spain Barcelona, Hospital of Santa Cruz [1960] Federal Republic of Germany Hamburger Kunsthalle / Federal Republic of Germany Museum Folkwang Essen / Switzerland Kunsthaus Zürich / Federal Republic of Germany Munich, Haus der Kunst [1961] France Paris, Musée Rodin / Netherlands Stedelijk Museum Amsterdam / Federal Republic of Germany Berlin, Akademie der Künste / Austria Vienna, Akademie der Bildenden Künste / Denmark Humlebaek, Louisiana Museum of Modern Art [1963] England Wakefield Art Gallery / England Hull, Ferens Arts Gallery [1964] Brazil Museu de Arte Moderna do Rio de Janeiro / Mexico Mexico City, Museo de Arte Moderno / Venezuela Museo de Bellas Artes de Caracas [1965] Argentina Buenos Aires, Museo Nacional de Bellas Artes [1966] Romania Bucharest, Sala Dalles / Czechoslovakia Bratislava, Slovak National Gallery / Czechoslovakia Prague, Národní Galerie / Israel Jerusalem, Israel Museum / Israel Tel Aviv Museum of Art [1967] Hungary Budapest, Műcsarnok / Ireland Dublin, Trinity College [1969] Japan Tokyo, National Museum of Modern Art / Japan Osaka, Hanshin Department Store / Japan Nagoya, Meitetsu Department Store [1970] Hong Kong Museum of Art [1971] Belgium Mechelen, Musée de Malines [1972] Italy Florence, Forte di Belvedere [1973] Luxembourg Musée d'État [1974] Scotland Edinburgh, Scottish Arts Council / Canada Toronto, Art Gallery of Ontario, Henry Moore Sculpture Centre [1977] France Paris, L'Orangerie des Tuileries [1981–82] Spain Madrid, Palacio de Velázquez y Palacio de Cristal, Parque del Retiro / Portugal Lisbon, Fundação Calouste Gulbenkian / Spain Barcelona, Fundació Joan Miró [1982] England Durham, DLI Museum and Arts Centre / Mexico Mexico City, Museo de Arte Moderno [1983] Venezuela Museo de Bellas Artes de Caracas [1986] Hong Kong Museum of Art and Visual Arts Centre / Japan Tokyo, Metropolitan Art Gallery / Japan Fukuoka Art Museum [1987] India New Delhi, National Gallery of Modern Art / Federal Republic of Germany Düsseldorf, Kunstsammlung Nordrhein-Westfalen [1988] England London, Royal Academy of Arts [1990] USSR Kiev, Ukrainian Museum of Fine Art [1991] Luxembourg Musée National d'Histoire et d'Art / Bulgaria Sofia, Cyril Methodius Foundation / Argentina Buenos Aires, Museo Nacional de Bellas Artes [1992] Australia Sydney, Art Gallery of New South Wales [1996] Germany Kunsthalle Mannheim / France Nantes, Musée des Beaux-Arts [1998] Austria Vienna, Kunsthistorisches Museum / England Norwich, Sainsbury Centre for Visual Arts [2000] China Beijing, China Art Gallery / China Guangzhou, Guangdong Museum of Art / China Shanghai Art Museum [2001] England London, British Council [2002] Germany Kunstmuseum Wolfsburg [2003] France Toulouse, Les Abattoirs [2004] Greece Athens, National Gallery / Romania Bucharest, National Museum of Art [2005] Brazil Pinacoteca de Estado de São Paulo / Mexico Mexico City, Museo Dolores Olmedo Patiño / Brazil Rio de Janeiro, Paço Imperial / Brazil Brasilia, Centro Cultural Banco do Brasil [2006] England Norwich Castle Museum and Art Gallery / England Sheffield, Millennium Galleries

Graham Sutherland Thorn Trees, 1945

Purchased November 1948
from Alex Reid & Lefevre for
£115 0s. 0d.
Oil on canvas, 127 × 101.5cm
P74

[1946] France Paris, Musée National d'Art Moderne [1947] Greece Athens, British Institute [1948] France Paris° / Sweden Stockholm, Konstförening / Australia Perth, Art Gallery of Western Australia [1949] Australia Brisbane, Queensland Art Gallery / Australia Adelaide, Art Gallery of South Australia / Australia Broken Hill Art Gallery / Australia Melbourne Royal Exhibition Building / Australia Sydney, Art Gallery of New South Wales / Australia Hobart, Tasmanian Museum and Art Gallery / Australia Launceston, Queen Victoria Art Gallery / Canada Toronto, Art Gallery of Ontario [1950] New Zealand Christchurch, Robert McDougall Art Gallery [1951] New Zealand Dunedin Public Art Gallery / New Zealand Wellington, National Art Gallery / New Zealand Auckland, City Art Gallery [1952] Italy Venice Biennale / France Paris, Musée Moderne de la Ville de Paris [1953] England London, Tate Gallery / Netherlands Stedelijk Museum Amsterdam / Switzerland Kunsthaus Zürich / Netherlands Stedelijk Museum Amsterdam / Switzerland Kunsthaus Zürich / Austria Innsbruck, Ferdinandeum [1954] Austria Vienna, Akademie der Bildenden Künste / Federal Republic of Germany Stuttgart° / Federal Republic of Germany Mannheim° / Federal Republic of Germany Berlin, Haus am Waldsee [1955] Federal Republic of Germany Hamburg° / Brazil São Paulo Bienal [1956] Norway Oslo, Kunstnernes Hus / Denmark Copenhagen, Kunstforeningen [1957] Japan Tokyo, Metropolitan Art Gallery [1958] Belgium Brussels° [1959] Northern Ireland Belfast Art Gallery [1960] USSR Moscow, Pushkin Museum of Fine Arts / USSR Leningrad, State Hermitage Museum [1962] Portugal Lisbon, Fundação Calouste Gulbenkian [1963] Iceland Reykjavik, National Museum / Canada Toronto, Art Gallery of Ontario [1964] Canada Musée des Beaux-Arts de Montréal / Canada Ottawa, National Gallery of Canada / Canada Winnipeg Art Gallery / Canada University of Regina, Norman Mackenzie Art Gallery / Canada Edmonton Art Gallery / Denmark Humlebaek, Louisiana Museum of Modern Art / Algiera Algiers, Musée du Bardot [1965] Italy Turin, Museo Civico [1966] Switzerland Kunsthalle Basel [1967] Federal Republic of Germany Munich, Haus der Kunst / Federal Republic of Germany Berlin° / Federal Republic of Germany Cologne° /

A NEO-ROMANTIC inspired by the pastoral subjects of Samuel Palmer, Graham Sutherland's haunting paintings express a revulsion at the machine age and the oppressive forces of industrialisation, by tackling the rugged, difficult beauty of the countryside. For much of the 1930s he would attempt to convey the intellectual and emotional essence of the Pembrokeshire landscape by means of dramatic shifts in light, unnaturalistic colouring and animal skulls. It is a bleak, primordial world in which man and nature are at odds with one another.

Sutherland had originally intended to study as a railway engineer, and perhaps it was his aborted education in this field that led him to look with such a distempered eye on the march of progress. His real development as a painter dates from 1935, when he visited Pembrokeshire in the Welsh border country, and began a series of paintings based on landscape and natural forms. In 'moments of vision', he felt that things were taking on a life of their own, and undergoing a metamorphosis from a static, fixed shape, to an undefined, indeterminate form. In his own words, he was fascinated by 'the whole problem of the tensions produced by the power of growth'. In 1940, he was employed by the War Artists Advisory Committee, established by the art historian Kenneth Clark. The aim was to record Britain at war, from bomb damage in the East End of London to tin mining in Cornwall and steel works in Cardiff. Discouraged from painting dead bodies, Sutherland would paint the skeletal remains of burnt-out buildings as a metaphor for human damage. Thorn Trees was made at the end of the war and Sutherland has chosen a palette of intense, cold colours to reinforce the impression of a cruel and unapprehending world. It is one of the of the final paintings he executed before fleeing the sulphurous realities of post-war Britain for the sunny environs of the South of France. The work was made after Canon Walter Hussey commissioned the artist to paint an altarpiece for his church in Northampton. Sutherland chose to paint the Crucifixion, and Thorn Trees was one of a number of paintings made shortly afterwards that focused on the crown of thorns pressed onto Christ's head by the soldiers. The picture transforms the trees into deadly weapons; the thorns become daggers and their razor-sharp edges glint like steel. Like a phoenix from the fire, this vicious aberration grows out of the barren soil, the mutant response to an evil world. JL

Netherlands The Hague° [1968] England London, British Council [1969] Japan Tokyo, British Council [1970] Japan Osaka, British Pavilion [1972] France Menton, Palais de l'Europe / England London, Whitechapel Art Gallery / England Southampton City Art Gallery [1973] England Carlisle Public Library, Museum and Art Gallery / England Durham, DLI Museum and Arts Centre / England Manchester City Art Gallery / England Bradford, Cartwright Hall [1975–76] England Sheffield, Mappin Art Gallery [1976] India New Delhi, National Gallery of Modern Art / India Bombay, National Centre for the Performing Arts [1977] New Zealand Auckland, City Art Gallery / New Zealand New Plymouth Art Gallery / Hong Kong Cultural Centre [1980] Norway Oslo, Kunstnernes Hus [1982] England London, Tate Gallery / Federal Republic of Germany Darmstadt° [1984] Federal Republic of Germany Recklinghausen° / England London, Serpentine Gallery [1987] England London, Barbican Art Gallery [1988] Switzerland Locarno° [1990] USSR Kiev, Ukrainian Museum of Fine Art [1991] Luxembourg Musée National d'Histoire et d'Art / Bulgaria Sofia, Cyril Methodius Foundation / Argentina Buenos Aires, Museo Nacional de Bellas Artes [1993] England Leeds City Art Gallery [1994] France Saint-Étienne, Musée d'Art Moderne [1995] Luxembourg Musée National d'Histoire et d'Art [1998] France Antibes-Juan-les-Pins, Musée Picasso [2002] Germany Kunstmuseum Wolfsburg [2003] France Toulouse, Les Abattoirs [2005] England London, Dulwich Picture Gallery / England Nottingham, Djanogly Art Gallery [2007] Belgium Ghent, Museum voor Schone Kunsten [2008] Syria Damascus, University of Damascus [2009] England Paddock Wood, Mascalls Gallery

Ben Nicholson 11 November 1947 (Mousehole), 1947

Purchased November 1948
from Alex Reid & Lefevre for
£170 0s. 0d.

Oil on canvas mounted on wood,
46.5 × 58.5cm

P78

[1949] England London, New Burlington
Galleries [1950] England London
University [1951] USA Washington,
Duncan Phillips Art Gallery [1953]
Sweden Göteborgs Konstmuseum,
Konsthall / Sweden Stockholm, Bildande
Konst [1954] Netherlands Stedelijk
Museum Amsterdam [1955] France
Paris, Musée National d'Art Moderne /
Belgium Brussels, Palais des Beaux-Arts /
Switzerland Kunsthaus Zürich / England
London, Tate Gallery [1956] Rhodesia
Salisbury, Rhodes Centenary Museum and
Art Gallery [1958] Iraq Baghdad* [1959]
Tunisia Tunis, Maison Associations
Culturelles [1960] Scotland Edinburgh,
Scottish National Gallery of Modern
Art [1961] Switzerland Kunsthalle
Bern [1962] England London, British
Council [1963] Hungary Budapest, Ernst
Múzeum [1964] Czechoslovakia Prague,
Uluv Exhibition Hall / Czechoslovakia
Bratislava, Mirbach Palace & Palffy Palace
/ Romania Bucharest, National Gallery
of Art / Romania Iaşi, Palace of Culture
[1969] England London, Tate Gallery
[1972] Norway Oslo, Kunstnerforbundet
/ Norway Trondhjiems Kunstforening /
Norway Bergen Kunstforening / Poland
Warsaw, Muzeum Narodowe / Poland
Poznań, Muzeum Narodowe / Poland
Kraków, Muzeum Narodowe / England
London, Whitechapel Art Gallery /
England Southampton City Art Gallery
[1973] England Carlisle Public Library,
Museum and Art Gallery / England
Durham, DLI Museum and Arts Centre
/ England Manchester City Art Gallery
/ England Bradford, Cartwright Hall
/ Scotland Aberdeen Art Gallery and
Museum [1977] France Les Sables-
d'Olonne, Musée de l'Abbaye Sainte-Croix
/ France Montbéliard, Musée du Château
/ France Rouen, Musée des Beaux-Arts
/ France Calais, Musée des Beaux-Arts
et de la Dentelle / France Bordeaux,
Galerie des Beaux-Arts [1978] France
Nantes, Musée des Beaux-Arts / France
Chartres, Musée des Beaux-Arts / USA
Buffalo, Albright-Knox Art Gallery /
USA Washington, Hirshhorn Museum
and Sculpture Garden [1979] USA New
York, Brooklyn Museum [1980] Wales
Swansea, Glynn Vivian Gallery [1985]
England London, Tate Gallery [1987]
Spain Madrid, Fundación Juan March
/ Portugal Lisbon, Fundação Calouste
Gulbenkian / England Penzance, Newlyn
Art Gallery / England London, Royal

BEN Nicholson's painting of a pretty, quiet harbour bay in
weathered hues of gold, magnolia and grey, is disrupted by large
abstract shapes that seem to float and hover in the plane. The bay
is the tiny harbour of Mousehole, pronounced 'Mowzel', which lies on
the coast of Cornwall; and those flat shapes included on the right-hand
side of the painting form elements of a still life. This part of the picture
is very similar to *1945 (still life)* (1945),[1] a sombre grouping of cups with
elegant looping handles, a bottle and perhaps some plates, which recalls
the Cubist arrangement of perspectives in the style of Georges Braque
or Pablo Picasso. Whilst marrying together two of Nicholson's preferred
genres of painting – still life and landscape – additionally, one can see
in this painting echoes of Nicholson's staunchly Modernist abstractions,
such as the spartan, monochrome 'White Reliefs' of squares and circles
that were begun in the 1930s.

What binds the incongruous elements in this painting together
are the colours and the textures of the paint. There is, unsurpris-
ingly, a marked contrast in the use of colour and light between
Nicholson's paintings in Cornwall, where he moved with his wife,
Barbara Hepworth, at the start of World War II, and those painted
in Cumberland in the north of England in the 1920s, which are dark,
bright and rich. *11 November 1947 (Mousehole)* typifies the palette for
which Nicholson's landscapes became best known: pale, golden and
ochre hues. These were undoubtedly affected by the light qualities
of the glinting Cornish sea and salt-blown countryside, and in this
painting the colours of the still life appear borrowed from the landscape.
Putty-coloured elements from the rocks and pavements around the harbour are seen on part of the bottle and several of the square, interlocking planes, along with the tones of chalky rocky white from the cliffs,
and other browns and golden sand colours from the earth. The sea, a
tone of whitish duck-egg blue, almost touching on amethyst in places,
reappears right at the centre of the still life's composition.

The textures, too, are significant, binding each of the separate
elements together. There are several areas of thin paint which appear
to have been roughly scrubbed away, so that the ruddy canvas shows
through. Whilst an emphasis on the handmade and craft tradition
may certainly have been influenced by Nicholson's relationship with
naïve painter Alfred Wallis, who lived nearby, this painting is a perfect
example of what Chris Stephens has termed Nicholson's 'domestication'
of the English landscape. Nicholson compared his manner of working
with the memory of his mother scrubbing the kitchen table, revealing
his determination 'to show that the making of art was ordinary and
domestic, as essential as housework'.[2] Bringing together the objects of
the home, and integrating them with the landscape, Nicholson human-
ises the sublime with small boats as part of an intimate, huddled scaling
that wraps itself around the viewer.

Since 1940, with *1940 (St Ives, version 2)*,[3] Nicholson had been
creating a series of works in which still life paintings were intertwined
with landscapes, generally using the device of a group of objects placed
near a window. In *Mousehole*, one might not, at first glance, recognise
the overlapping foreground shapes as still life objects – it simply looks
as though elements of the landscape have come forth and arranged
themselves into a new vortex of physical forms, or abstract impressions.
This notion might be illuminated by Nicholson's comment some years
later: 'All the "still lifes" are in fact land-sea-sky scapes to me.'[4] LMF

College of Art / France Saint-Étienne,
Musée d'Art Moderne [1989] Japan
Hyogo Prefectural Museum of Modern
Art / Japan Kamakura, Museum of
Modern Art / Japan Tokyo, Setagaya
Art Museum [1990] USSR Kiev,
Ukrainian Museum of Fine Art [1991]
Luxembourg Musée National d'Histoire
et d'Art / Bulgaria Sofia, Cyril Methodius
Foundation / Argentina Buenos Aires,
Museo Nacional de Bellas Artes [1992]
Belgium Brussels, Breydel building, EEC
Commission [1993] England London,
Tate Gallery [1994] France Saint-Étienne,
Musée d'Art Moderne / England London,
British Council [1998] France Colmar,
Musée d'Unterlinden [2002] Spain
Valencia, IVAM Centre Julio González
/ Germany Kunstmuseum Wolfsburg
[2003] France Toulouse, Les Abattoirs /
England Penzance, Penlee House Gallery
and Museum / England Lincoln, Usher
Gallery / England Doncaster Museum
and Art Gallery [2004] Japan Hayama,
Museum of Modern Art / Japan Nagoya,
Aichi Prefectural Museum of Art / Japan
Tokyo Station Gallery [2005] Oman
Muscat, British Council [2007] Belgium
Ghent, Museum voor Schone Kunsten
[2008] Syria Damascus, University of
Damascus / England Kendal, Abbot Hall
Art Gallery / England Bexhill-on-Sea, De
La Warr Pavilion [2009] England Tate
St Ives

1. Tate Collection, London.

2. Chris Stephens, introduction to *A
Continuous Line: Ben Nicholson in
England*, exh. cat. (London: Tate, 2008),
12.

3. The Phillips Collection, Washington,
DC.

4. Letter from Nicholson to Patrick
Heron (9 February 1954), quoted in
Jeremy Lewison, *Ben Nicholson*, exh. cat.
(London: Tate Gallery, 1993), 86.

Purchased December 1948
from The London Gallery
for £157 10s. 0d.
Oil on canvas, 106 × 75cm
P79

KITTY, the daughter of Jacob Epstein and Kathleen Garman, reappears in Lucian Freud's portraits over the course of five years – clutching a kitten, head under leaves or on the pillow – but from the outset *Girl with Roses* establishes a scale and ambition that is life-size. She and Freud married in February 1948, and in the same year, Freud spent a whole train journey with Pablo Picasso's *Weeping Woman* (1937),[1] taking it down to Brighton for an exhibition. Picasso wrenches the woman's head apart, as if viewing her from inside out, through her own tears; Freud answers this visual outburst by observing how emotion manifests itself on the outside. Newly pregnant, Kitty sits stiffly, her eyes averted in a dead stare. She clutches a rose, and another lies limp in her lap. A yellow-pink breed, renamed the 'Peace Rose' at the end of the war, it is more than the traditional love token and, like the glimmer of Kitty's teeth, adds a hint of menace. Titian's fleshy *Venus of Urbino* (1538)[2] is recast for a cold climate of woollies and rations.

Kitty's grip on the rose is matched by Freud's grip on the brush. Lawrence Gowing infers a kind of passive purity in Freud's early style – the linearity, thin application of paint and cool palette – and applauds its 'homogenous, even legibility and a sea-washed cleanliness', yet here the subject's vitality is picked out with needling precision.[3] From the stray curls across the forehead to the tweezered eyebrows, the reflection of a sash window in each eye, the frayed cane of the chair and the birthmark on the raised hand, ultimately the 'girl' of the title becomes Kitty in the definite article. Freud explains, 'I was trying for accuracy of a sort. I didn't think of it as detail. It was simply, through my concentration, a question of focus. I always felt that detail – where one was conscious of detail – was detrimental.'[4]

Girl with Roses is as much a love portrait of Freud's painter heroes as of Kitty. It unfolds from the rose at its centre, a nod to the straightforward flower paintings of Cedric Morris, under whom Freud studied at the East Anglian School of Painting and Drawing (1939–42). Petals rebound in the pale twist of Kitty's lips, the bloom of her skirt, and finally the ochre folds in the background, which call to mind Jean Dominique Ingres. Freud admits, 'You get really excited about an Ingres fold in a curtain because you don't think that so much can be said in such an incisive and economical way.'[5] Indeed, the 'Ingres of existentialism' (Herbert Read's tag) invokes the great dress of *Madame Moitessier* (1856)[6] with Kitty's sweater. Its ribbed neck and cuffs and gently contoured stripes (black stippling was a tip from advertising, to make the green buzz) are defined incisively and economically – an understanding of fabric perhaps aided by a commission to create designs for dress fabrics for Asher (London) Ltd in 1946. In a statement published in *Encounter* to coincide with his selection for the XXVII Venice Biennale (1954), Freud explains, 'The effect in space of two different human individuals can be as different as the effect of a candle and an electric light bulb. Therefore the painter must be concerned with the air surrounding his subject as with the subject itself.'[7] So, Kitty is viewed in prickly proximity, a halo of individual hairs reach out from her head, nervy with static. DF

1. Tate Collection, London.

2. Uffizi, Florence.

3. Lawrence Gowing, *Lucian Freud* (London: Thames & Hudson, 1982), 81.

4. William Feaver, 'Beyond Feeling', Freud in conversation with Feaver, in *Lucian Freud*, exh. cat. (Sydney: Art Gallery of New South Wales, 1992), 12.

5. Freud quoted in William Feaver, *Lucian Freud* (New York: Rizzoli, 2007), 321.

6. The National Gallery, London.

7. Lucian Freud, 'Some thoughts on painting', *Encounter*, 3/1 (July 1954), 23–24.

Purchased February 1950
from The Lefevre Gallery
for £475 0s. 0d.
Rosewood on wooden base,
height 100.3cm
P167

The shapes we are creating are not abstract, they are absolute.
Naum Gabo, 1937[1]

BARBARA Hepworth was a practitioner of direct carving, and resonating through *Rhythmic Form* are various rhythms: those of the artist at work, of the work in space, and of the context of its production. Alan Wilkinson has described the shape of *Rhythmic Form* as a 'soaring upright'.[2] It has all the grace of Brancusi's *Bird in Space* (1927),[3] and yet it is hewn from the land, shaped in such a way as to create a spatial bond between place, form and the inner creative spirit of the artist. For Hepworth, sculpture was the 'plastic projection of thought' – a way of translating ideas that can only be expressed through direct and spontaneous acts of engagement with a material in order to arrive organically at something whole and complete.[4] Once finished, the work can then stand by itself, its power lying in the fact that, as she wrote in 1937, it 'puts no pressure on anything'.[5]

Hepworth's earliest sculptures were largely figurative. During the 1930s, having visited the studios of Arp and Brancusi whilst in Paris, and under the influence of Nicholson, Moore, Gabo and other members of the Unit One group in London, her work took on a greater level of abstraction. The human figure was re-imagined and taken in new directions exploring scale, poise, and natural form. Wilkinson has argued that seeing the work of Arp generated what was to become for Hepworth 'a life-long obsession – the almost mystical identification with the human figure and human spirit inhabiting the landscape'.[6] In 1937, the critic J. D. Bernal compared her sculpture to 'the Neolithic Menhirs which stand through Cornwall and Brittany as memorials to long forgotten dead' and whose stones were pierced so as to 'furnish a means of egress for the soul'.[7] In 1939, at the invitation of critic Adrian Stokes, Hepworth left London for Carbis Bay, just outside St Ives, travelling with her husband, Ben Nicholson, and their three children. The area was to play a key role in Hepworth's work, and later sculptures frequently referred to local sites.

Another recurring motif in Hepworth's sculpture is the hole. It is a powerful gesture of both creation and amputation that can be seen as a resolutely feminine act of empowerment. It is like an eye that has bored right through the wood, uniting both sides of the work and endowing it simultaneously with asymmetry, incision and cohesion. Another technique, first prompted by Moore's figures of the late 1930s, was to incorporate string. Works such as *Pelagos* (1946)[8] and *Wave* (1943)[9] are good examples of this, and it can also be seen developed in later bronze sculptures such as *Winged Figure*, which adorns the John Lewis Partnership building on Oxford Street, London, inaugurated in April 1963. The sense of a dynamic equilibrium between competing shapes and asymmetries is crucial to Hepworth. As she states, 'Asymmetry can be found in the tension, balance, inner vital impact with space and in the scale'.[10] Within this tension is held the 'inner force and energy' between 'thought and medium', which gives the work its lasting vital presence. R P

1. Naum Gabo, 'Sculpture and
Construction in Space', in J. L. Martin,
Ben Nicholson and N. Gabo (eds.), *Circle*
(London: Faber and Faber, 1937), 109.

2. Alan G. Wilkinson, 'The 1930s:
Constructive Forms and Poetic Structure',
in Penelope Curtis and A. G. Wilkinson,
Barbara Hepworth, exh. cat. (London:
Tate Gallery, 1994), 64.

3. Museum of Modern Art, New York.

4. Barbara Hepworth, 'Sculpture', in *Circle*
(1937), 114.

5. Ibid., 116.

6. Wilkinson, 'The 1930s', 45.

7. Ibid., 62.

8. Tate Collection, London.

9. National Galleries of Scotland,
Edinburgh.

10. Hepworth, 'Sculpture', 114.

Purchased December 1961
from the artist for £500 0s. 0d.
Oil on Masonite, 121.9 × 243.8cm
P345

[**1963**] Australia Sydney, British Council
[**1967**] Federal Republic of Germany
Munich* [**1968**] England London, Tate
Gallery / England Plymouth City Museum
and Art Gallery / England Newcastle,
Laing Art Gallery / England Birmingham
City Museum and Art Gallery / England
Liverpool, Walker Art Gallery [**1978**]
England Manchester, Whitworth Art
Gallery / Scotland Glasgow, Kelvingrove,
Art Gallery and Museum / England
Cambridge, Kettle's Yard / England
Bristol, Royal West of England Academy
[**1985**] England London, Tate Gallery
[**1987**] France Saint-Étienne, Musée
d'Art Moderne [**1989**] Japan Hyogo
Prefectural Museum of Modern Art /
Japan Kamakura, Museum of Modern
Art / Tokyo Setagaya Art Museum
[**1990**] USSR Kiev, Ukrainian Museum
of Fine Art [**1991**] Luxembourg Musée
National d'Histoire et d'Art / Bulgaria
Sofia, Cyril Methodius Foundation /
Argentina Buenos Aires, Museo Nacional
de Bellas Artes [**1992**] England London,
Camden Arts Centre [**1993**] England
Coventry, Mead Gallery / England
Sheffield, Mappin Art Gallery / England
Penzance, Newlyn Art Gallery [**1995**]
Wales Cardiff, National Museum of Wales
[**1997**] Cyprus Nicosia Municipal Arts
Centre [**1998**] Ireland Dublin, Royal
Hibernian Academy [**1999**] Spain A
Coruña, Fundación Pedro Barrié de la
Maza / Spain Ciudadela de Pamplona /
Netherlands Amstelveen, Cobra Museum
voor Moderne Kunst / Spain Salamanca,
Palacio de Abrantes / Spain Barcelona,
Centre Cultural de Caixa Terrassa /
Spain Jerez, Sala Pescadería Vieja [**2000**]
England Tate St Ives [**2003**] Croatia
Zagreb, British Council

1. <http://collection.britishcouncil.
org/html/work/work.
aspx?a=1&id=42990&section=/artist/>
accessed February 2009.

2. William Feaver, 'Introduction', in Peter
Lanyon and Andrew Lanyon, *Cornwall*
(Penzance: Alison Hodge, 1983), 5.

3. Museum of Modern Art, New York.

4. Andrew Causey, *Peter Lanyon* (London:
Bernard Jacobson, 1991).

THE abstract landscapes of Peter Lanyon upturn the rigours of perspective, exploiting the colour and texture of paint to burrow into the gritty layers of meaning present within his native Cornish homeland. Neither scenic nor picturesque nor figurative, Lanyon worked into the paint his emotive engagement with places he knew well, providing immediate portraits of their character that are both tightly lyrical and distinctly raw in their execution. In a talk he gave for the British Council in 1962 about *Bojewyan Farms*, Lanyon described the 'bucolic … rather earthy' scene in the ancient village of Bojewyan, just outside St Just in Cornwall.[1] Lanyon was able to elaborate the complexity of place through the surface of the canvas, evoking something of its character through motifs, gestures and mood. In this way he might be compared to artists such as Paul Nash, Graham Sutherland and Ivor Hitchens, who were seeking to go beyond the mere outward appearance of a setting to communicate what lies behind and within it. In being so strongly tied to one area it would be easy to dismiss Lanyon's work as parochial, but there is a technical mastery and latent consciousness in the bond he has with Cornwall which evidently goes beyond this, as William Feaver has pointed out: 'The true landscapist, whether a Constable or a Cézanne, is rarely at home, so to speak, in more than one place. Lose sight of your roots and you become displaced and relatively superficial.'[2]

Lanyon was fortunate to have roots in an area that had, as a result of the onset of war, become one of the main centres of British avant-garde art, with its hub in St Ives. Having briefly attended art schools in Penzance and then the Euston Road School, Lanyon was also fortunate to be taken under the wing of Ben Nicholson, who had moved to the coastal town with his wife, Barbara Hepworth, in 1939. Lanyon's visual education was interrupted, however, by the outbreak of hostilities, and he served in the RAF for the duration of the Second World War. There is a sense of urgency and an emphasis on sensation that give his paintings an immense charge, a quality no doubt heightened by the experiences and situations encountered while on active service. Most importantly, there is an understanding of the landscape as if from the air (in 1959 he became a gliding enthusiast).

Nicholson had taught Lanyon how to think abstractly in terms of space and form, and how to imbue these with ideas. By the late 1940s and early 1950s, whilst the paintings of St Ives by Nicholson had a certain classical thinness, Lanyon's resonated a rich energy. During this time, he was starting to see the work of the American Abstract Expressionists, including the mature Willem de Kooning at the Venice Biennale of 1950 and later Jackson Pollock's *One (No. 31)* (1950)[3] when it was shown at the ICA in 1953. Andrew Causey has described how Lanyon was able to reinvent himself.[4] His introduction to prominent New York artists (he later met Rothko in 1957) undoubtedly opened new possibilities and freedoms in his work, and led to four solo shows there. Lanyon's career was tragically cut short when he died in a gliding accident in 1964. RP

Victor Pasmore
Abstract in White, Black, Brown and Lilac, 1957

Purchased March 1960
from the artist for £700 0s. 0d.
Relief construction (painted
wood), 95.3 × 102.9cm

P325

[**1960**] Italy Venice Biennale / Yugoslavia Belgrade, Art Pavilion [**1961**] England London, ICA / France Paris, Musée des Arts Décoratifs / Netherlands Stedelijk Museum Amsterdam / Federal Republic of Germany Städtische Kunstgalerie Bochum / Belgium Brussels, Palais des Beaux-Arts / Belgium Liège, Association pour le Progrès Intellectuel et Artistique de la Wallonie / Norway Oslo, Kunstnernes Hus [**1962**] Denmark Humlebaek, Louisiana Museum of Modern Art [**1963**] Iceland Reykjavik, National Museum / Canada Toronto, Art Gallery of Ontario [**1964**] Canada Ontario, London, Public Library / Canada Musée des Beaux-Arts de Montréal / Canada Ottawa, National Gallery of Canada / Canada Winnipeg Art Gallery / Canada University of Regina, Norman MacKenzie Art Gallery / Canada Edmonton Art Gallery / Denmark Humlebaek, Louisiana Museum of Modern Art [**1965**] Brazil São Paulo Bienal [**1966**] Venezuela Museo de Bellas Artes de Caracas / Brazil Museu de Arte Moderna do Rio de Janeiro / Chile Santiago, Museo de Arte Contemporáneo / Peru Lima, Instituto de Arte Contemporáneo [**1968**] India New Delhi, Lalit Kala Akademi [**1972**] Norway Oslo, Kunstnerforbundet / Norway Trondhjiems Kunstforening / Norway Bergen Kunstforening / Poland Warsaw, Muzeum Narodowe / Poland Poznań, Muzeum Narodowe / Poland Kraków, Muzeum Narodowe [**1974**] Federal Republic of Germany Cologne, British Council [**1997**] Cyprus Nicosia Municipal Arts Centre [**1998**] Ireland Dublin, Royal Hibernian Academy [**1999**] Spain A Coruña, Fundación Pedro Barrié de la Maza / Spain Ciudadela de Pamplona / Netherlands Amstelveen, Cobra Museum voor Moderne Kunst / Spain Salamanca, Palacio de Abrantes / Spain Barcelona, Centre Cultural de Caixa Terrassa / Spain Jerez, Sala Pescadería Vieja [**2002**] Germany Kunstmuseum Wolfsburg [**2003**] France Toulouse, Les Abattoirs [**2005**] Oman Muscat, British Council

MADE a decade after what Herbert Read hailed as a 'revolutionary' departure from representational painting, *Abstract in White, Black, Brown and Lilac* presents a cross section of Victor Pasmore's core concerns. It epitomises his 'notion of constructing a picture like a carpenter constructs a box with wood, saw, hammer and nails'.[1] The rectangular support is divided by a central spine from which painted wooden strips reach out on either side and forward into the viewer's space. Shifting back and forth in three dimensions, it seems it could almost melt through the wall. This kind of carpentry invokes the mysterious as much as the workmanlike.

The dominant terminology around Pasmore's 'conversion' to abstraction implies that this was a decision of bewildering, spiritual magnitude.[2] Yet this relief shows abstraction to be – far from a split – a logical step from his figurative period, as founding member of the Euston Road School. 'Most remarkable of all,' Norbert Lynton maintains, 'he was not afraid to risk the comment that he had not gone abstract after all but merely shifted the balance of observation.'[3] Its deceptively unobtrusive palette (the coloured forms *do* protrude) can be traced back to scenes of the Thames, such as *Quiet River* (1943–44)[4] or *Hanging Gardens of Hammersmith No.2* (1949),[5] where branches and posts hover or recede in indeterminately anaemic water, air, mist; Pasmore, a conscientious objector, caught the chill in the air as Britain awaited reconstruction.

Looking back, he regarded it as an inevitability that 'the implications of modern scientific development would affect the imagery of naturalist art as drastically as they altered the concepts of natural philosophy'.[6] D'Arcy Wentworth Thompson's classic biology text, *On Growth and Form* (2nd ed., 1942), presents a mathematical analysis of natural forms determined by their growth patterns, and it is a reference point for the post-war Constructivist revival, with Pasmore at the helm. Yet if his underlying concepts were scientific in inspiration, his work was instinctive in practice, allowing for what Lawrence Alloway called 'delicate, hunchy' decision-making. In 1956, Alloway observed Pasmore at work in his Blackheath studio and described the systematic process that went into a similar relief.[7] Investigation of a rectangle was initiated by sketches of horizontal and vertical lines, which were adapted to a specific rectangle taken from a textbook. Plastic and plywood strips were arranged on a sheet of glass above a large white baseboard on the floor, culminating in a spec. for production (often in batches) in a London factory.

The inquiry into formal boundaries between painting, sculpture and architecture underpinned Pasmore's teaching as Head of Painting at King's College, Newcastle, where his and Richard Hamilton's 'Basic Form' course ('each category should be presented as part of a developing process') was set to become a national model.[8] At the same time, as design consultant for Peterlee New Town in County Durham he could expand his methods on an environmental scale. His Apollo Pavilion, a network of concrete slabs intersecting over a lake (completed 1970), was to prove a magnet for graffiti, which he deemed a humanising addition. Likewise, despite the regularity of machine-made right angles, flush intersections and even surfaces in *Abstract in White, Black, Brown and Lilac*, there is a resistance to its being overly 'finished'. Playing with optical assumptions, it bulges with a sense of 'almost': the rectangular mount is *almost* square, the linear forms flanking the spine are *almost* inversely symmetrical. And as the white mount bleeds into the larger plane of the surrounding wall, so too the painted forms gesture towards the expanse off-limits, like lines of text inviting a page to be turned.   DF

1. Victor Pasmore, 'The Transformation of Naturalist Art and the Independence of Painting', in Alan Bowness and Luigi Lambertini, *Victor Pasmore: with a Catalogue Raisonne of the Paintings, Constructions and Graphics, 1926–1979* (London: Thames & Hudson, 1980), 100.

2. See for example Jasia Reichardt, *Victor Pasmore* (London: Methuen, 1962), unpaginated.

3. Norbert Lynton, *Victor Pasmore: Nature into Art*, exh. cat. (New York: Center for International Contemporary Arts, 1990), 26.

4. Tate Collection, London.

5. Tate Collection, London.

6. Victor Pasmore, *Victor Pasmore: Recent Works 1974–77*, exh. cat. (London: Marlborough Fine Art, 1977), 3.

7. Lawrence Alloway, 'Pasmore Constructs a Relief', *Art News*, 55/4 (Summer 1956).

8. Victor Pasmore, 'A Developing Process in Art Teaching', in *The Developing Process* (Durham: University of Durham, 1959), 3.

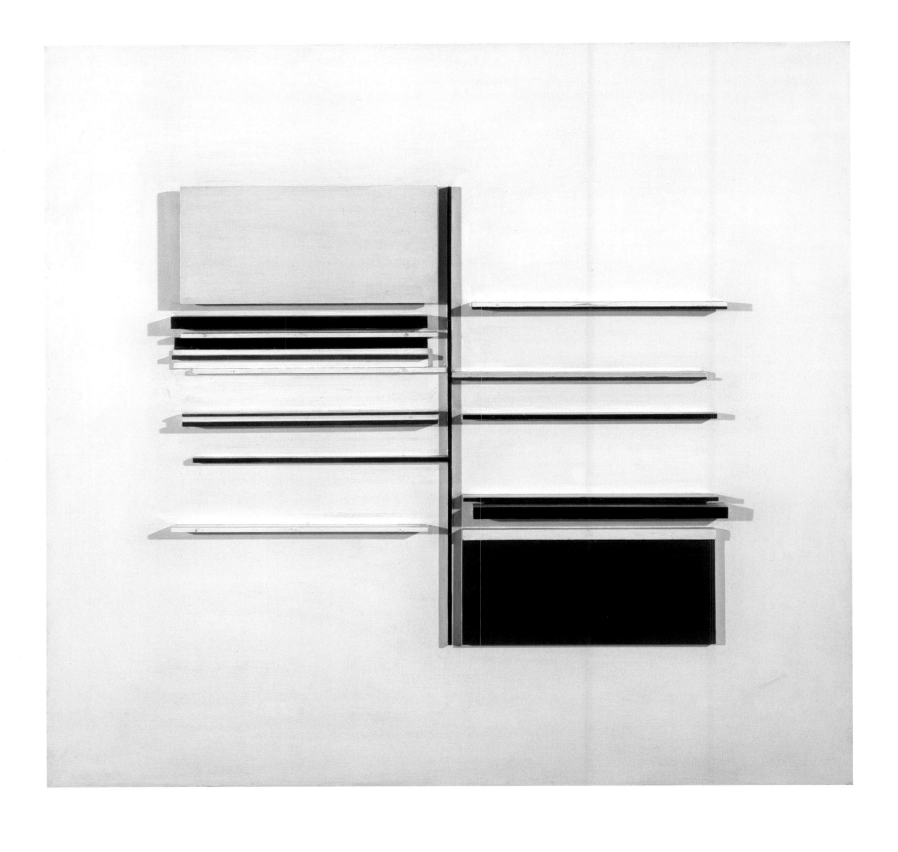

David Hockney
Man in a Museum (or You are in the Wrong Movie), 1962

Purchased August 1971 from
R. B. Meyer, Chicago, for $12,000
Oil on canvas, 147.3 × 152.4cm

P1494

DAVID Hockney had just graduated from the Royal College of Art, and was enjoying a new wave of confidence; it was at this time, he felt, 'I became aware as an artist.'[1] That summer, in an article for *Ark*, the RCA journal, Dick Smith remarked, 'Hockney as a personality is bound up with his paintings. The paintings serve as letters, or diary jottings or mementoes; the figures *are* portraits; events portrayed *did* happen.'[2] Meanwhile, Hockney was en route to Italy with his friend, Jeff Goodman, when just such an event gave rise to the seminal sequence of paintings among which the present piece is counted. On a visit to the Pergamon, Berlin, they got separated. Hockney recalls, 'Suddenly I caught sight of him standing next to an Egyptian sculpted figure, unconcerned about it because he was studying something on the wall. Both figures were looking the same way, and it amused me that in my first glimpse of them they looked united.'[3] Drawings made back in the hotel room served as the basis for *The First Marriage*[4] and *Picture Emphasizing Stillness*,[5] as well as *Man in a Museum (or You are in the Wrong Movie)*.

In this chance conjunction then, the restless graduate spotted a comic reincarnation of Sickertian ennui. A man on the left stands in full profile, looking at something off-canvas. The paint barely covers the body, and an initial attempt at a profile is left showing through the ankles (working in oils at the time, Hockney would draw straight from brush to canvas). Trousers are merely suggested and the primrose jacket fades into raw canvas background – a pointer to Francis Bacon, or Ron Kitaj, Hockney's great friend from the RCA. Meanwhile, a large Egyptian figure sits to the right, its head turned to look at the man, or perhaps the same artwork off-stage. The Egyptian is more thoroughly realised. It is busy with different graphic marks – red and blue scribbles, a weathered cummerbund and bold stripes around the collar. With luscious lips, a golden sweep of hair and arms akimbo, it makes a prime stand-in for B-movie beefcake or, equally, a bored wife having a sit-down.

The alternative title, *You are in the Wrong Movie*, is retained in parentheses, raising textual eyebrows at the absurdity of the coincidence. It also suggests that somewhere out there is the *right* movie set. Hockney gets a kick from the flagrantly artificial, just as the illustrations in American nudist and gay magazines, 'obviously (like old movies) shot in the made-up sets out of doors', were to be a window onto a bright-buffed world out of England.[6]

The museum setting also serves to place this specific 'memento' within Hockney's larger concerns as to his place among peers, both contemporaneous and historical. 'I think I've had a permanent affair with the art of the past and it goes hot and cold; the art of the past can be treated too pompously … The truth is, the art of the past is living; the art of the past that has died is not around.'[7] Pooh-poohing pomposity, *Man in a Museum* literalises the idea of an artwork being alive, and gives it eyes that can follow you round the room. Hockney exults in the bizarreness of assuming a relationship with the art of the past, by turns touching, droll, creepy – as the overarching theme of the 'Marriage' series implies, it is only as odd as many human relationships.   DF

1. Hockney quoted in Nikos Stangos (ed.), *David Hockney by David Hockney* (London: Thames & Hudson, 1976), 66.

2. Richard Smith, 'New Readers Start Here…', *Ark*, 32 (Summer 1962), 38.

3. *David Hockney by David Hockney*, 89.

4. *The First Marriage (A Marriage of Styles I)* (1962), Tate Collection, London.

5. 1962, Private collection.

6. Hockney quoted in Christopher Finch, *David Hockney in America*, exh. cat. (New York: William Beadleston, 1983), unpaginated.

7. *David Hockney by David Hockney*, 87.

Purchased November 1969 from
Hanover Gallery for £2,500 0s. 0d.
Welded and painted aluminium,
height 162.6cm

P1273

[**1969**] Sweden Göteborgs Konstmuseum,
Konsthall [**1970**] Netherlands The Hague,
Gemeentemuseum [**1976**] Canada
Saskatchewan, National Exhibition Centre
/ Canada Vancouver, Fine Arts Gallery
[**1977**] Canada Hamilton, McMaster
University Art Gallery / Canada Musée
des Beaux-Arts de Montréal / Canada
Edmonton Art Gallery [**1978**] Poland
Various venues [**1979**] South Africa
Various venues [**1981**] Hong Kong
Museum of Art [**1983**] Spain Barcelona,
Departament de Cultura, Generalitat
de Catalunya / Spain León, Caja de
Ahorros / Spain Zamora, Casa de la
Cultura / Spain Vigo, Caja de Ahorros
[**1984**] Greece Various venues / Scotland
Edinburgh, Royal Scottish Academy
[**1985**] France Lyon, Musée Saint Pierre
Art Contemporain / Ireland Cork,
Crawford Art Gallery [**1990**] USSR Kiev,
Ukrainian Museum of Fine Art [**1991**]
Luxembourg Musée National d'Histoire
et d'Art / Bulgaria Sofia, Cyril Methodius
Foundation / Argentina Buenos Aires,
Museo Nacional de Bellas Artes [**1992**]
Ghana Accra, British Council [**1994**]
Russia St Petersburg, State Russian
Museum [**1995**] Russia Moscow, New
Tretyakov Gallery / Czech Republic
Prague Castle, Riding School [**1996**]
Morocco Casablanca, Espace Wafabank
/ Germany Museum Folkwang Essen
/ France Calais, Le Channel, Galerie
de l'Ancienne Poste [**1997**] Pakistan
Karachi, Hindu Gymkhana / Pakistan
Lahore, The Old Fort [**1998**] South Africa
Johannesburg Art Gallery / South Africa
Cape Town, South African National
Gallery / Zimbabwe National Gallery
Bulawayo [**1999**] Zimbabwe Harare,
National Gallery of Zimbabwe / France
Valenciennes, Musée des Beaux-Arts
[**2000**] Cyprus Nicosia Municipal Arts
Centre / Malta Valletta, St James Cavalier
Centre for Creativity [**2001**] France
Paris, Centre Georges Pompidou [**2002**]
Germany Kunstmuseum Wolfsburg

EDUARDO Paolozzi was born of Italian parentage in Leith, Scotland.
He had grown up working after school and on weekends in the
family sweet shop, where his father used to collect and fix up old
radios. Amidst this earnest and hard-working environment one gets
the sense that the young Paolozzi was fascinated by the colourful array
of temptation that surrounded him: the comics and magazines, the
sweet wrappers and no doubt the sweets themselves. The fantastically
gaudy colours of *Diana as an Engine I* surely owe something to this
environment, albeit refracted through his education and development
as a Surrealist intellectual with his eyes open to the visual languages
of the day. (It is notable that in a conversation with J.G. Ballard in 1971,
Paolozzi said, 'What I like to think I'm doing is an extension of radical
Surrealism.'[1])

Diana as an Engine I follows on from the exhibition 'This is
Tomorrow', the apex of the Independent Group's achievements, staged
at the Whitechapel Art Gallery in 1956. The show consisted of twelve
exhibits, each multi-disciplinary in spirit, being designed jointly by
a different team comprising a painter, a sculptor, and an architect.
Some exhibits showed more explicitly Constructivist and Surrealist
tendencies, whilst others had a more techno-futurist feel, extrapolating
contemporary trends in science fiction.[2] The future, in a world in which
atomic annihilation was an ever-present possibility, was a refuge for the
imagination, offering a space where the latent impulses of the present
could be taken beyond their temporal and logistical limits. The country
had only just come off rationing, and the incorporation of the ephemera
of American mass culture raised tantalising possibilities: perhaps
British culture could also be opened to the consumer urges and libidinal
excitements emanating from across the Atlantic.[3] In 1952, Paolozzi had
famously delivered a lecture-cum-slideshow he titled 'bunk', in which
he played out a sequence of images drawn from a variety of sources
including magazines, postcards, Modernists, adverts and tribal cultures.
'History is bunk', he seemed to say, following the famous dictum of
Henry Ford, and so is 'high' art – but that is where its meaning and
significance can be found, by placing it alongside everything else from
the standpoint of today.

Diana as an Engine I is a feverish but controlled fusion of form and
cultural ephemera: a mélange that appears to incorporate such diverse
inspirations as an American fire hydrant, a New York taxi cab lost in
Vegas, a steam train, the exhaust of a convertible, a whirlygig lollypop
and an early off-the-wall idea for a Dalek. And yet it feels wrong to even
try to situate this work, since Paolozzi was not about to indulge in the
Western habit of ordering and compartmentalising its vision. Perhaps it
is better to see it as a shining totem of unbridled consumer fetish, cast
within a field of mesmeric visual stimuli.   RP

[**2003**] France Toulouse, Les Abattoirs
[**2004**] Iran Tehran, Museum of
Contemporary Art / Romania Bucharest,
National Museum of Art [**2005**] Greece
Andros, Basil and Elise Goulandris
Foundation Museum of Contemporary
Art / Portugal Lisbon, British Council
[**2007**] Italy Rome, Scuderie del Quirinale
[**2008**] Portugal Lisbon, British Council

1. Paolozzi quoted in Keith Hartley,
'Introduction', *Paolozzi* (Edinburgh:
National Galleries of Scotland, 1999), 9.

2. See Hal Foster, Rosalind Krauss,
Yve-Alain Bois and Benjamin H. D.
Buchloh, *Art Since 1900: Modernism,
Antimodernism, Postmodernism* (London:
Thames & Hudson, 2004), 385–90.

3. Anne Massey, 'Forbidden
Conversations: The Independent Group,
Modernism, urban reality and American
mass culture', in *Blast to Freeze: British
Art in the 20th Century* (Ostfildern: Hatje
Cantz, 2002), 139–44.

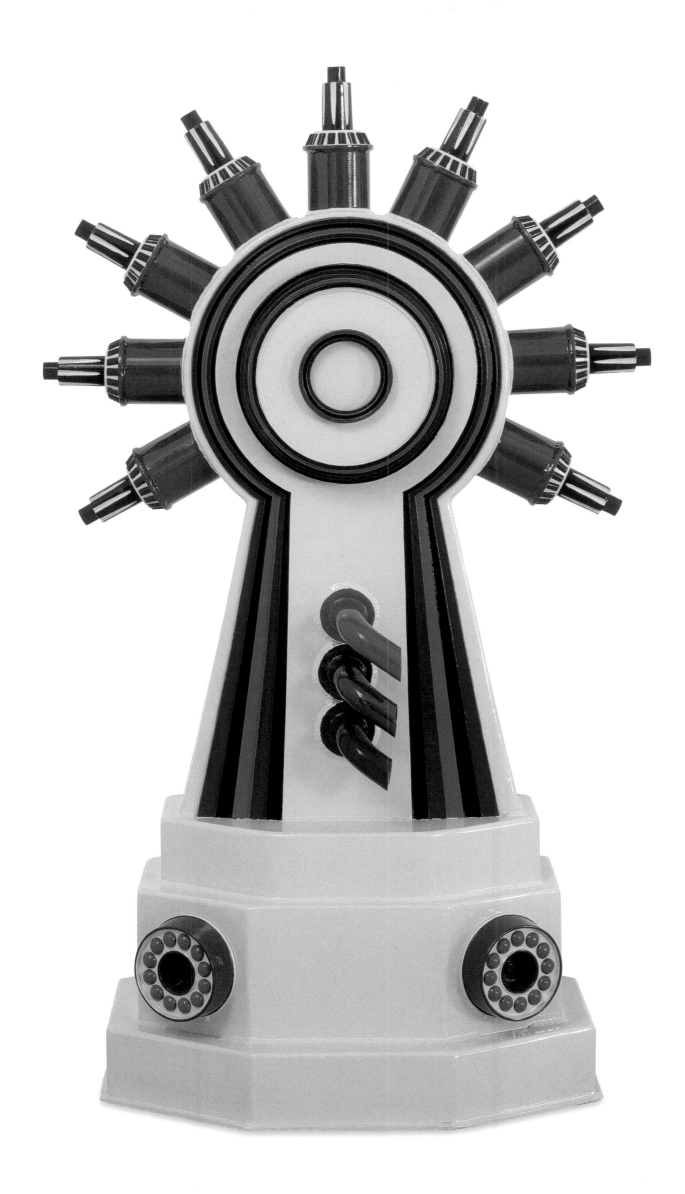

Purchased March 1969
from Waddington Galleries
for £500 0s. 0d.
Alkyd on hardboard,
122 × 213.4cm

P1241

[1968] Federal Republic of Germany
Berlin, Akademie der Künste [1969]
Federal Republic of Germany Dortmund,
Museum am Ostwall / Federal Republic
of Germany Kunstverein Hannover
/ Austria Vienna, Museum des 20
Jahrhunderts [1970] USA Washington,
National Gallery of Art [1972] Norway
Trondhjiems Kunstforening / Norway
Oslo, Kunstnerforbundet / Norway
Bergen Kunstforening / Poland Kraków,
Muzeum Narodowe [1978] Japan Tokyo,
Seibu Museum of Art [1990] USSR Kiev,
Ukrainian Museum of Fine Art [1991]
Luxembourg Musée National d'Histoire
et d'Art / Bulgaria Sofia, Cyril Methodius
Foundation / Argentina Buenos Aires,
Museo Nacional de Bellas Artes [1992]
England London, British Council [1995]
France Paris, British Council [2000]
India New Delhi, British Council

1. Marco Livingstone, 'Perspectives
on Painting: Seven essays on the art of
Patrick Caulfield', in *Patrick Caulfield*,
exh. cat. (London: Hayward Gallery,
1999), 13.

2. Caulfield in dialogue with Bryan
Robertson, in *Patrick Caulfield* (1999), 24.

3. Letter from Caulfield to Andrea Rose
(March 1990), quoted in *For a Wider
World: Sixty Works from the British
Council Collection*, exh. cat. (London:
British Council, 1990), 88.

4. Private collection.

5. Private collection.

6. Manchester Art Gallery, and Museo
Nacional de Arte Reina Sofia, Madrid,
respectively.

7. Caulfield quoted in Marco Livingstone,
Patrick Caulfield: Paintings (Aldershot &
Burlington: Lund Humphries, 2005), 19.

8. Dialogue with Bryan Robertson, 25.

9. Christopher Finch, 'The Paintings of
Patrick Caulfield', *Art International* (20
January 1966), 49.

10. Dialogue with Bryan Robertson, 28.

11. The J. Paul Getty Museum,
Los Angeles.

AT over two metres across, *View Inside a Cave* has its mouth wide open; the viewer's eye is swallowed by an even expanse of two-tone grey, guided by cartographical lines around the path's swerve to the right. As Marco Livingstone remarks, 'One cannot fail to be reminded of the simple perspectival devices featured in how-to-draw manuals.'[1] Early on, as a student, Patrick Caulfield made the impersonal surface and graphic outline – the stuff of a million billboards – his particular hallmark: 'This was my reaction against the Englishness of English painting which so greatly valued a slightly understated, tentative figuration.'[2]

View Inside a Cave joins a series of paintings from Caulfield's years immediately after the Royal College of Art, all done in an ostentatiously landscape format and given the prefix 'View'. A partly ironic title, he confirmed, as it was precisely the 'flat shadowless manner that denied the recessive expectations of a view'.[3] In these paintings, Caulfield cocks a snook at the institutionalised *plein-air* by seeking the nearest thing to indoors, from *View of the Ruins* (1964)[4] and *View of the Rooftops* (1965)[5] to the snug boltholes *Inside a Weekend Cabin* and *Inside a Swiss Chalet* (both 1969).[6] An urban aesthetic of street signs and natty packaging is transferred out of town. Experience tells, from an early job in the design department of Crosse & Blackwell and a term in the commercial art department at Chelsea School of Art, which equipped Caulfield with armaments against the 'misty brush strokes' that prevailed in academic art of the time. 'It seemed a reason to use very crisp black lines.'[7]

The black lines that so clean up the cave's crags and gravel can also be related to Caulfield's first trip abroad, to Crete in the summer between leaving Chelsea and starting at the RCA. He was wowed by the liberally restored palace at Knossos, where 'the terracotta red and black contrasts seemed Japanese or at least oriental; the vividness of colour and sharp contours struck me quite forcibly'.[8] Caulfield had a magpie eye for the vivid, and 'crude' Touristico postcards were as exciting as Fernand Léger's bold objects or Hergé's *Adventures of Tintin*. It was this embrace of visual sources high and low that saw him lumped with the Pop movement – a cause of irritation to Caulfield, who maintained his work shared none of Pop's 'social realism'.

In *View Inside a Cave* exactitude combines with an absence of detail to create an enveloping atmosphere by disarmingly economic means. Indeed Christopher Finch's memorable phrase for Caulfield – 'a romantic disarmed by his own irony' – directs our attention to the poetry of Jules Laforgue.[9] Caulfield, a fan since college days, uses words such as 'succinct', 'condensed', 'crisp', and 'pungent' to describe Laforgue's imagery, words that equally apply to his own.[10] Nowhere more so than in his treatment of the cave, a subject not without weighty precedent. A century before, Gustave Courbet had confronted the refined style and strictures on subject matter that ruled academic painting with his fantastically crusty caves, such as *Grotto of Sarrazine* (1864),[11] where the paint is almost sculpted, and the cave's mouth curls round like an Atlantic breaker, affirming the concrete reality of an empty landscape. As if in subdued reference, Caulfield chooses to paint on the slightly rougher reverse side of the hardboard. He has put both subject and style through the refinery, distilling the atmosphere of emptiness. Graceful, raffish even, *View Inside a Cave* leads us on. Behind it, echoes of man's primeval art; ahead, we can only guess the next frame. DF

Purchased February 1968 from
Rowan Gallery for £1,400 0s. 0d.
PVA emulsion on linen,
221.9 × 222.9cm
P996

[**1968**] Italy Venice Biennale / Federal
Republic of Germany Städtische
Kunstgalerie Bochum [**1969**] Netherlands
Rotterdam, Museum Boijmans Van
Beuningen / Japan Tokyo, National
Museum of Modern Art [**1970**] Austria
Vienna, Wiener Secession [**1970–71**]
Federal Republic of Germany Kunstverein
Hannover / Switzerland Kunsthalle Bern
/ Federal Republic of Germany Kunsthalle
Düsseldorf / Italy Turin, Galleria Civica
Moderna / England London, Hayward
Gallery / Czechoslovakia Prague, Národní
Galerie [**1973**] France Paris, Musée d'Art
Moderne de la Ville de Paris / England
Manchester, Whitworth Art Gallery /
England Sheffield, Mappin Art Gallery /
England Durham, DLI Museum and Arts
Centre / Scotland Edinburgh, Scottish
National Gallery of Modern Art / England
Birmingham City Museum and Art
Gallery / England Letchworth, Museum
and Art Gallery / England Bristol, City
Art Gallery and Arnolfini Gallery [**1977**]
England London, Royal Academy of Arts
[**1978**] USA Buffalo, Albright-Knox Art
Gallery / USA Dallas, Museum of Fine
Arts [**1979**] USA Purchase, Neuberger
Museum of Art / Australia Sydney,
Centrepoint Gallery Space / Australia
Perth, Art Gallery of Western Australia
[**1980**] Japan Tokyo, National Museum
of Modern Art [**1984**] England London,
Serpentine Gallery [**1990**] USSR Kiev,
Ukrainian Museum of Fine Art [**1991**]
Luxembourg Musée National d'Histoire
et d'Art / Bulgaria Sofia, Cyril Methodius
Foundation / Argentina Buenos Aires,
Museo Nacional de Bellas Artes [**1993**]
Spain Madrid, British Council [**1996**]
England London, Independent Art
Space / England Southampton, John
Hansard Gallery / England Manchester,
Cornerhouse [**1997**] England London,
Institute of Contemporary Arts / England
Tate St Ives [**1999**] England London,
Serpentine Gallery / Germany Düsseldorf,
Kunstverein für die Rheinlande und
Westfalen [**2000**] USA New York, Dia
Center for the Arts [**2001**] Germany
Galerie für Zeitgenössische Kunst
Leipzig [**2002**] Germany Kunstmuseum
Wolfsburg [**2003**] France Toulouse, Les
Abattoirs / England London, Tate Britain /
Austria Kunsthaus Graz [**2004**] Australia
Sydney, Museum of Contemporary Art
[**2005**] New Zealand Wellington, City
Art Gallery / Switzerland Aarau, Aargauer
Kunsthaus [**2008**] France Paris, Musée
d'Art Moderne de la Ville de Paris

MADE in the run-up to the XXXIV Venice Biennale (1968), where she was the first British artist (and first woman) to win the International Prize for Painting, the 'Cataract' series marked a defining moment in Bridget Riley's career. 'Colour presented a crisis for me,' she admitted. 'If you think of a square, a circle, or a triangle, no matter what size it may be, you know exactly what form you can expect to see.'[1] After six monochrome years, epiphany: 'I saw that the basis of colour was its instability.'[2]

Although Riley had in fact been making colour studies since 1961, these didn't make it to final pieces until grey emerged as a conduit for colour into the black and white situation. 'Instability' was accommodated by a departure from distinctive geometric shapes and a significant increase in scale. In *Cataract 3*, a pair of coloured stripes unfurl like ribbons across the white canvas, broadening and thinning in shallow curvilinear sequences – stripes, edge-rich, maximise chromatic interaction. Although on a minute level these colours can be identified as vermilion and turquoise (warm and cold extremes), the painting revels in its lack of fixity. The curves undulate diagonally, as if a gentle south-west wind were blowing across a silk sheet, but on another level light crackles at different speeds and in ungovernable directions. Pigment is transformed into an active condition, in which true engagement with the painting is to see 'a luminous disembodied light, variously coloured'.[3]

Cataract 3 is a multi-focal revelation, in inverse proportion to the disabling effects of an ophthalmological cataract – the clouding of the eye's lens. Nevertheless, towards the centre of the painting the chromatic contrast heightens, leaving an impression of a radiant swathe between the upper and lower reaches, which are increasingly grey. The eye is guided, then tripped up; it should feel many things, Riley hopes, 'caressed and soothed, experienc[ing] frictions and ruptures, glide and drift'.[4] Rhythms and counter-rhythms enact the title's other meaning, a furious rush of water that foams white through the force of its own impact. Indeed the entire field is saturated with movement, and such immersion recognises a pedigree of influences, including Monet's *Water Lilies* (1916)[5] and Cézanne's *Mont Sainte-Victoire* (1902–04).[6]

Riley has been at pains to spell out that 'nature is not a starting point somewhere outside my work which then leads me into doing it'.[7] Somewhat misleading, perhaps, in a celebrated essay, 'The Pleasures of Sight', she describes formative memories from a Cornwall childhood, notably the 'narrow dark streaks of ruffled water – violets, blues and many shades of grey – as a sudden squall swept over the sea'.[8] Although this image bears a striking resemblance to the present piece, it did not serve as source material. Instead it serves to highlight the vital quality of visual experience: 'surprise'. Riley's method is to concentrate on small studies at the preparatory stage – the decision-making – and leave final execution to assistants. Consequently, the finish of *Cataract 3* is smooth and understated, in order that, as Robert Kudielka suggests, 'the *literal* surface recedes behind the foreground of perception'.[9] This may be diagrammatically tidy, but it is not a scientific analysis. Maurice de Sausmarez identifies the dialectic: 'On the one hand in her work the means are ordered, precise and controlled to the maximum, while on the other, the end is free, vibrating and dynamic.'[10] Light is allowed to play the chameleon.   DF

1. Riley in interview with Michael Craig-Martin, in *Bridget Riley: Selected Paintings 1961–1999*, exh. cat. (Düsseldorf: Hatje Cantz, 2000), 68.

2. Riley in dialogue with Michael Craig-Martin, in Robert Kudielka (ed.), *Bridget Riley: Dialogues on Art* (London: Zwemmer, 1995), 56.

3. Riley in conversation with Robert Kudielka (1972), in Paul Moorhouse (ed.), *Bridget Riley*, exh. cat. (London: Tate, 2003), 209.

4. Bridget Riley, 'The Pleasures of Sight' (1984), in Moorhouse (ed.), 213–14.

5. National Museum of Western Art, Tokyo.

6. Philadelphia Museum of Art.

7. Riley in conversation with Isabel Carlisle, *Bridget Riley: Works 1961–1998*, exh. cat. (Kendal: Abbot Hall Art Gallery, 1998), 7.

8. Riley, 'The Pleasures of Sight', 213–14.

9. Robert Kudielka, *Bridget Riley: Works 1959–78*, exh. cat. (London: British Council, 1978), 3.

10. Maurice de Sausmarez, *Bridget Riley* (London: Studio Vista, 1970), 90.

Richard Hamilton The Solomon R. Guggenheim (White), (Black), (Chromium), 1970

Purchased May 1972 from
Nigel Greenwood for £54 each
(White), *(Black)* painted
plastic, *(Chromium)* chromed
plastic, three reliefs each
70.5 × 70.5 × 15cm
P1537, P1538 & P1539

[**1974**] France Toured under the auspice
of the Direction-Générale des Musées
Classés [**1975–76**] Luxembourg° [**1977–
78**] Netherlands° [**1978**] Germany°
/ Austria° [**1981**] Cyprus° / Tunisia°
[**1982**] Iraq° / Japan° / Singapore°
[**1983**] Philippines° / Korea° [**1985**]
Israel° / Yugoslavia° [**1986–87**] Senegal°
/ Zimbabwe° [**2003**] Estonia Tallinn,
Museum of Contemporary Art [**2004**]
Armenia Yerevan, National Gallery /
Kazakhstan Almaty, Central Exhibition
Hall / Romania Constanţa Art Museum
/ Romania Bucharest, National Museum
of Art / Romania Iaşi, Palace of Culture /
Romania Timişoara, Faculty of Fine Arts
/ Romania Cluj, Biblioteca Judeţeană
Octavian Goga / Italy Rome, Istituto
Nazionale per la Grafica [**2005**] Portugal
Porto, Culturgest / Lithuania Šiauliai
Art Gallery [**2006**] Poland Kraków,
Manggha Centre / Taiwan Taichung,
National Taiwan Museum of Fine Arts /
Taiwan Taipei, Kundu Museum of Fine
Arts [**2007**] China Chongqing, Tank Loft
/ Ireland Letterkenny, Glebe House and
Gallery [**2008**] Poland Warsaw, Zachęta
Gallery

THE 'Guggenheim Reliefs' bolster Richard Hamilton's position at the
bookends of Pop Art in Britain. With *Just What Is It That Makes
Today's Homes So Different, So Appealing?* (1956),[1] a tiny collage
for the Independent Group exhibition 'This is Tomorrow', Hamilton
had provided an index to everything British Pop Art was to explore.
Acclaimed and spurred on by the younger generation of artists emerging
from the Royal College – Peter Blake, Patrick Caulfield, David Hockney,
Derek Boshier, Allen Jones et al. – Hamilton's work from the latter half of
the 1960s went from strength to strength. By 1970, always fascinated by
new technology, Hamilton was redirecting advances in product design
into fine art, with the backing of xartcollection, Zurich, a young company
that pioneered the production of multiples with the aim of bringing art
to a wider audience.

In the mid-1950s, Hamilton had looked away from Britain, still
overshadowed by post-war austerities, to America, a beacon of glam-
our, prosperity, possibility. Yet he did not actually visit America until
1963, after which he asked Lawrence Alloway, then curator at the
Guggenheim Museum of Modern Art, New York, to send photographs
of Frank Lloyd Wright's building, already an icon just a few years after
its opening. These provided the starting point for Hamilton to work
through a simulation of the architectural process, 'from visualisation of
the building to the planning to construction and even later to photo-
graphing and publicising'.[2] The concept of environmental art – as seen
in Hamilton's collaboration with Alloway and Victor Pasmore on 'An
Exhibit' (1957)[3] – is turned inside out. Instead of starting with the artwork and working outwards to engage with a space, the Guggenheim
Reliefs start with a work of architecture and condense it into a cast. The
present series is a triple exclamation mark in black, white and chrome,
punctuating the original set of drawings, prints and six fibreglass reliefs.[4]
It was thought that the high cost of creating the moulds would be offset
by producing a large edition of 750. In the event, the project was unex-
pectedly difficult and the edition stopped at 271. (Xartcollection went
bust in 1973.)

Hamilton addresses his own question, 'Does the neutrality of
Duchamp or the studied banality, even vulgarity, of the subject-matter
in most American Pop Art significantly exclude those products of mass
culture which might be the choice of a NY Museum of Modern Art
"Good Design" committee from our consideration?'[5] He controls the
Guggenheim's assertive presence by not only engineering a false perspective for the reliefs (suggesting concentric circles rather than a winding
spiral), but also colouring each relief differently, fishing for new associations. The fibreglass series had been painted in tints derived from postcards, whereas colour was innate to the material of the vacuum-formed
trio, and redolent of new-fangled goods, from sex-shop-black, to wash-
ing-machine-white and the chromium plating of a brand-new toaster.
Hamilton is providing the kind of range to be expected from any good
retailer, and in so doing, ties bows with what Reyner Banham saw as a
'cordon sanitaire' between architecture and pop art – the 'deep seated
desire by the profession that architecture remain a humane "consultant"
service to humanity, not styling in the interests of sales promotion'.[6] It is
no coincidence that vacuum forming was by 1970 the acme of standard
product packaging. The Guggenheim Reliefs imply that a museum is
the ultimate packaging for the ultimate consumable (fine art). They also
convert that packaging into an art product. So impressed was Hamilton
by the Guggenheim that it literally bulges through in his work, while the
exhibition context finds itself reflected in the reliefs' shiny surfaces. DF

1. Kunsthalle Tübingen.

2. Richard Morphet, *Richard Hamilton*,
exh. cat. (London: Tate Gallery, 1970), 67.

3. Curated by Hamilton, Alloway and
Pasmore, 'An Exhibit' was shown at the
Hatton Gallery, Newcastle, and the ICA,
London.

4. The series was first exhibited in 1966 at
the Robert Fraser Gallery, London.

5. Richard Hamilton, *Collected Words
1953–1982* (London: Thames & Hudson,
1982), 72.

6. Reyner Banham, 'Towards a Pop
Architecture', *Architectural Review* (July
1962), quoted in David Robbins (ed.), *The
Independent Group: Postwar Britain and
the Aesthetics of Plenty* (Cambridge, MA:
MIT Press, 1990), 175.

Purchased March 1973
from Rowan Gallery for £360
Acrylic on canvas, 274.4 × 183cm
P1588

[**1973**] **France** Paris, Musée d'Art
Moderne de la Ville de Paris [**1974**]
France Menton, Palais de l'Europe [**1990**]
USSR Kiev, Ukrainian Museum of Fine
Art [**1991**] **Luxembourg** Musée National
d'Histoire et d'Art / **Bulgaria** Sofia, Cyril
Methodius Foundation / **Argentina**
Buenos Aires, Museo Nacional de Bellas
Artes [**1992**] **Ireland** Dublin, Irish
Museum of Modern Art [**2004**] **England**
London, BBC

CHINESE legend has it that between you and your loved one, across eternity, there lies an unbreakable red thread. *Red Light* was one of the first paintings to establish Sean Scully's reputation, winning him the John Moores Prize in 1972. With hindsight, Scully draws a thread back to the unified simplicity of Rothko's favourite painting, *The Red Studio* (1911) by Matisse.[1] But back in the early 1970s, his intention was to 'make a mystery or a compression of a surface', and his compass points were Pollock (freedom, desire) and Mondrian (attuned geometry).[2] Scully tackles the colour red by constructing a psychedelic scaffolding, drawing the eye into an illusion of space through a dense grille of thin stripes, blue, canary yellow, pink, umber, bottle green, apricot. It is a noisy, luminous profusion that builds up over shadowy reaches behind and scatters the gaze every which way. Red light has the longest wavelength in the spectrum visible to the human eye, on the cusp of infrared. Notice the red horizontals, the last to be applied, sitting quietly on the top layer, like the warming filaments of an electric heater.

Scully's early work is systematic. Clean, hard edges are achieved by means of a lot of masking tape. He would mark up a grid, lay masking tape onto the canvas, apply paint (acrylic), then another set of masking tape lines, more paint with heavy rollers, and so on until the canvas was filled up, a panel of taut plaid. He only stopped when information that had been put down was being taken away. Architectural, these grid structures lend *Red Light* the soaring verticality of a skyscraper, anticipating perhaps Scully's move from Newcastle to New York, Greenbergian terrain, in 1975 (he turned to oils at that point). William Feaver, then a Newcastle neighbour, conveys the wow effect: 'It followed a rigid, two-to-the-bar rock and roll beat, so overdubbed and multi-tracked that, rather like one of Phil Spector's multitudinous, pop sound-barrier breaking record productions, the best of the completed paintings overcame colour barriers and, as Scully puts it, "became totally organic. So that the painting was not simply a demonstration of process."'[3]

More than a demonstration of process, *Red Light* harbours personal preoccupations. 'Nothing is abstract: it's still a self portrait.'[4] From a rough childhood in South London, Scully had moved to study and teach at Newcastle University (1968–72). It was a singular time, when Newcastle enjoyed a distinct scene of its own, associated with Victor Pasmore and Richard Hamilton ('I had heard of Richard Hamilton, and was happy he wasn't there'[5]) as well as Bryan Ferry. Scully's red thread takes in the all-over-ness of his tutor Ian Stephenson's drip-drop atmospheres, the overlapping frisson of steel girders bridging the Tyne, and the 'low optical hum' of Bridget Riley.[6] Often described as unashamedly modern, Scully's avowed disinterest in fashion, even at this nascent stage, feeds into a preoccupation with Britishness. He stresses Britain's island position – in physical, temperamental and aesthetic terms – in between Europe and America. It is 'desirable but difficult to invade. The Spanish Armada was chased all around the coast of Britain and Ireland, by sailors who understand that navigation (the ability to blow with the wind) was more important than big guns. It was that chase that caused the Armada to self-destruct incrementally, detail by detail. And it is this space that exists between the border of things that has made the British character'.[7] The idea of the border of things is paramount in *Red Light*. Scully navigates the elusive inlets, stripe-to-stripe, with brawny nimbleness.   DF

1. Museum of Modern Art, New York.

2. Sean Scully, 'The Phillips Collection Lecture' (2005), in *Resistance and Persistence, Selected Writings* (London: Merrell, 2006), 165.

3. William Feaver, 'Sean Scully', *Art International* (December 1973), 26.

4. Sean Scully, 'Zurich' (2006), in *Resistance and Persistence*, 78.

5. Sean Scully, 'Ian Stephenson, Man of the North' (2005), in *Resistance and Persistence*, 100.

6. Sean Scully, 'High and Low, or the Sublime and the Ordinary' (1989), in *Resistance and Persistence*, 18.

7. Scully, 'Ian Stephenson, Man of the North', 104.

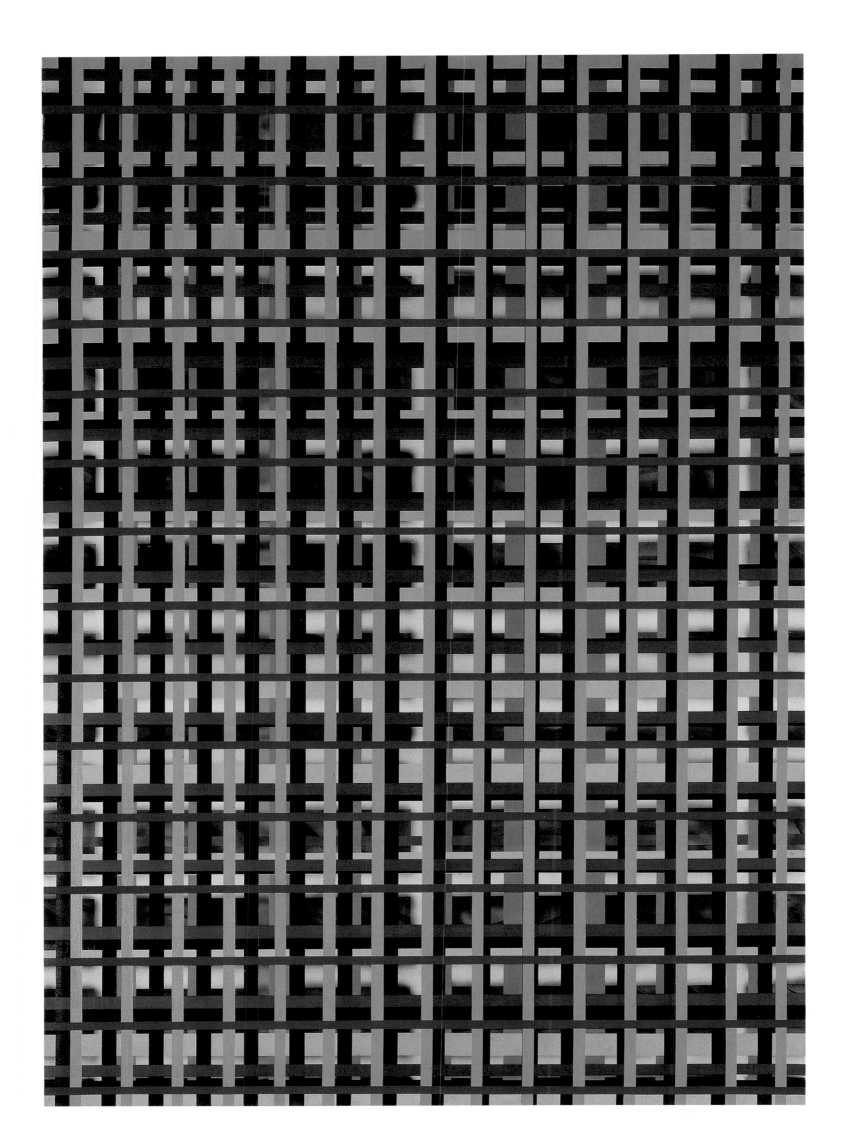

Purchased June 1983
from Browse & Darby for £12,000
Oil on canvas, 83.8 × 111.8cm

P4343

[**1989**] Malaysia Kuala Lumpur, National Art Gallery [**1990**] Hong Kong Museum of Art / Singapore The Empress Place Gallery / Zimbabwe Harare, National Gallery of Zimbabwe [**1991**] England London, British Council [**1992**] England London, Sotheby's / Israel Jerusalem, Israel Museum [**1993**] Singapore British Council [**2000**] Mexico Mexico City, Museo de Arte Moderno / Mexico Museo de Arte Contemporáneo de Monterrey [**2001**] Romania Bucharest, British Council [**2003**] Wales Flintshire, Buckley Library / Wales Llanwrst, Hafod Centre / Wales Denbigh Library Museum and Art Gallery / England Kendal, Abbot Hall Art Gallery [**2004**] England London, British Council [**2006**] Croatia Zagreb, British Council

A WOMAN reclines in glowing white, her posture a combination of relaxed elegance and studied, thoughtful tension, pressing together index finger and thumb on each hand. Although we have a full view of her face, she is looking outside the field of the canvas – dark eyes staring into the middle distance.

Whilst Euan Uglow's studies of nudes are among his best-known works of the 1970s, the portrait *Georgia* has both a tonal quality and an engagement with the subject that sets it apart from the colder objectivity of the nudes. The palette is soft, yet bright – colours rich with grey and violet – accentuated by the boldly patterned teal and pale honey fabric upon which she rests. Painting marks – pale areas of thinner paint, of grids and crosses – can be seen, mainly focused around the outline that separates the model from the wall behind her. Here, the image's cohesion is occasionally torn into, giving us a glimpse of the grid on which the paint sits. The area around the head and arms in particular seems to shimmer with the movement around the white fabric, which spills into the atmosphere, causing the model's figure to advance and recede against the deep dove-coloured wall behind her. As Myles Murphy has commented,

The answer to the question of what is the object, is that everything is. … There are two structures here, as there are in the Italian landscapes: the one of the imagery and space and the accompanying one across the surface – structures which are usually so close, one so overlays the other, that they are accepted as one and the same, but these later paintings are a reminder that the coinciding is a matter of arrangement and that they are capable of a separate and independent existence.[1]

The model is Georgia Georgallas, a longtime friend of Uglow, who began posing for him on Saturdays while she was a student at Camberwell Art College, where he taught. In this painting Georgia is wearing a long-sleeved Manchester United football shirt, with distinctive red and white striped cuffs and neckline, taken in to create a short mini dress. She also wears shiny Mary Quant tights dyed pink, and a special 'cupless bra' that the artist sent Georgia to buy from a corsetière in Knightsbridge.[2] When first looking at the painting, the viewer's gaze is caught by the face, tripping over the barely held breasts to the stomach – an area of gentle luminosity – calm and gently rounded. It is on the stomach that the brightest white light is focused, in a long, soft oval, which assists the tactile impression of weight and rest. 'We instinctively feel', writes Richard Kendall, 'the support for the woman's body in the buoyant upholstery and understand the muscular contrast between her solemnly held head and her lightly poised fingers.'[3]

LMF

1. Myles Murphy quoted in Catherine Lampert, *Euan Uglow: The Complete Paintings* (New Haven: Yale University Press, 2007), 121.

2. Ibid., 120.

3. Richard Kendall, 'Euan Uglow: Eye, Hand and Mind', in *Euan Uglow: Controlled Passion*, exh. cat. (Kendal: Abbot Hall Gallery, 2003), 8.

Purchased February 1977
from Fischer Fine Art for £777.60
Oil on board, 36.2 × 61cm

P3069

[1985] England London, British Council
[1992] Israel Tel Aviv, British Council
[1997] Portugal Lisbon, Fundação
Calouste Gulbenkian [1998] France Paris,
Musée Maillol [1999] England London,
British Council [2001] Portugal Lisbon,
British Council

RAILWAY lines are the veins and arteries of a view that Leon Kossoff cultivated from a studio in Dalston Lane, which he occupied between 1972 and 1975. 'London, like the paint I use, seems to be in my bloodstream. It's always moving – the skies, the streets, the buildings. The people who walk past me when I draw have become part of my life.'[1] Having grown up in the East End, he is measuring out familiar ground in terms of intense proximity. From the studio window, *View of Dalston Junction* swoops over a dense body of structures, heaved close to each other, like passengers packed into a railway carriage – houses to branches, girders to telegraph poles, sky to rooftops, grass to topsoil. One budge and everything is affected.

It was not until the late 1960s, after a decade of un-peopled building sites and no-go railway areas, that figures began to enter Kossoff's cityscapes, and here there is a passer-by, boxed into the foreground. In an essay for Kossoff's exhibition at the XLVI Venice Biennale (1995), David Sylvester applauds the instinctive grandeur of the atmosphere: 'The artist convinces us that he has merely drawn out a quality that was inherent in the figures or the places.'[2] That figure is a siphon into the place, making grandeur accessible. Tapping into the innate quality of a place is an ethos instilled by David Bomberg, whose life class at Borough Polytechnic Kossoff attended once a week for two years (1950–52). He recalls the energetic concentration of the class; for him and his friend Frank Auerbach, Bomberg's teaching was a crucial supplement to studies at St Martin's. *View of Dalston Junction* is grounded in Bomberg's axiom, 'drawing is sculpturally conceived in the full, like architecture'. It could, in fact, be seen as sculpturally-conceived drawing-in-paint. Hence the use of hardboard, rather than canvas: basic stuff, it copes with a lot of paint, built up and scraped off, leaving the traces from which to start improvising again, until the image is clinched.

Kossoff's titles often draw attention to the specifics of time, place, season; for example, from the same period, *Demolition of the Old House, Dalston Junction, Summer* (1974),[3] *Dalston Junction with Ridley Road Street Market and Salmon Curer's Yard, Friday Morning* (1973),[4] or *Dalston Lane, Monday Morning, Spring* (1974).[5] At less than a third of their size, the intimate scale of *View of Dalston Junction* adds to the sense that the landscape is not just a place, passive, to be inhabited, but a living, breathing character in itself. It is something to live *with*, actively. In a letter to John Berger, Kossoff explained: 'The subject is visited many times and lots of drawings are made, mostly very quickly. The work is begun in the studio where each new drawing means a new start until one day a drawing appears which opens up the subject in a new way, so I work from the drawing as I do from the sitter.'[6] On this particular day in 1975, Rembrandt, Constable, Van Gogh and Giacometti are invited to take a lungful of Dalston air – nippy, gleaming, potent city air. Here, as elsewhere, Kossoff's colours are capricious, morphing across a streaked and pitted surface (Rudi Fuchs notes they 'glow the way colours glow in the dusk').[7] Texts about his work have accrued a certain vocabulary of 'thickness' and 'heaviness' over the decades, but extract the paintings from linguistic sediment and what they contain is a very particular, mutable light. They demand long-looking. They radiate a zeal for staying power.   DF

1. Kossoff quoted in Paul Moorhouse, *Leon Kossoff*, exh.cat. (London: Tate Gallery, 1996), 36.

2. David Sylvester, 'Against the Odds', in *Leon Kossoff: Recent Paintings*, exh. cat. (London: British Council, 1995), 16.

3. Tate Collection, London.

4. National Gallery of Australia, Canberra.

5. Private collection.

6. Correspondence between Kossoff and John Berger, *The Guardian* (1 June 1996), 29.

7. Rudi Fuchs, 'Leon Kossoff', *Leon Kossoff: Recent Paintings* (1995), 22.

Purchased December 1976 from
Marlborough Fine Art for £1,800
Oil on board, 35 × 38.1cm

P3050

[**1977**] England London, British Council
[**1984**] England London, Serpentine
Gallery / India New Delhi, Lalit Kala
Akademi [**1985**] India Bombay, National
Centre for the Performing Arts [**1986**]
England London, British Council [**1987**]
USA San Bernardino Art Museum / USA
Santa Cruz County Museum [**1988**] USA
Sonoma State University / USA Santa
Barbara Museum of Art [**1990**] England
London, British Council [**1996**] Italy
Rome, British Council

FRANK Auerbach corrects the comparison between art and travelling: 'It's not a question of a protean adventurer – the traveller's unaltered and what he sees changes. Likewise the artist is the man in front of the writing-pad or in front of the easel, and things around him change and he doesn't change – that's the connection.'[1] Auerbach has worked in the same studio since taking it over from his friend and fellow Royal College student, Leon Kossoff, in 1954. Just over the way, on the junction of Camden High Street, Mornington Crescent and Crowndale Road, the Camden Theatre is another stayer. It opened on Boxing Day 1900, and has seen out over a century of bombs, demolition, and passing trends, playing host to the music hall, cinema, BBC radio, all-night parties and pop concerts, through assorted reincarnations (the Palace Theatre, the Camden Hippodrome, the Music Machine, the Camden Palace, Koko). It is on the periphery of a network of theatres designed by W. G. R. Sprague, whose ice-cream architecture (cloudy pastiches of Georgian, Baroque and Louis XVI styles) pervades the West End, a London peculiar.

Auerbach derives a compost of delicious surprises from 'this higgledy-piggledy mess of a city', and has returned to the Camden Theatre repeatedly.[2] More than the lump sum of its walls and angles, a haptic understanding of the theatre and its environs is translated, oil and board, into something organic. Auerbach illustrates his ambition in painting with reference to Robert Frost: 'A great painting is like ice on a stove. It is a shape riding on its own melting into matter and space, it never stops moving backwards and forwards.'[3] Here, the theatre is a watery façade, its pillars and copper dome blotted out in a lachrymose haze, quivering all over with the tangibility of its relation to other things. Tomato purée zigzags streak across the road in the foreground, straight from the tube. High street and pavement, hot orange and chocolate daubs, ooze in contact with the cool breeze of sky. Auerbach admires the loose body of English paintings in the National Gallery, as if 'it was arrived at empirically, out of sensation, as though there is a sort of fresh wind blowing through a room of English painting.'[4] The same wind blows through *The Camden Theatre*, airing out the theoretical. Its surface – like a finger pushing through cooling jam – ripples with sensory experience.

When he first moved to London in 1947, aged 16, Auerbach's dreams of being an actor were superseded by art classes at the Hampstead Garden Suburb Institute and, under David Bomberg, at Borough Polytechnic. As an artist his process was to have all the rigour of method acting. Starting with morning drawings on the spot, he paces through lines of charcoal, crayon or pencil just as actors pace through their lines each evening, in an attempt to make each performance new. He limbers up for the act of painting, a performance reserved for the studio, establishing an image then scraping it off, maybe many times in a single session, for up to eight hours. 'It is very much a question of rehearsing until one *becomes* the part, the object, the subject.'[5] Although these landscapes, as in *The Camden Theatre*, often take a smaller scale than the portraits, they are feats of exertion. They meet that persistent exhortation from another great fan of the music hall, Rudyard Kipling:

> *If you can make one heap of all your winnings*
> *And risk it on one turn of pitch-and-toss,*
> *And lose, and start again at your beginnings*
> *And never breathe a word about your loss* 'If...' iii.1–4

DF

1. Auerbach in conversation with Catherine Lampert, *Frank Auerbach*, exh. cat. (London: Arts Council of Great Britain, 1978), 13.

2. Auerbach in interview with Judith Bumpus, *Art & Artists* (June 1986), 27.

3. Auerbach in conversation with Lampert (1978), 20.

4. *Frank Auerbach and the National Gallery* (London: National Gallery, 1995), 16.

5. Auerbach quoted by Lawrence Gowing, 'Introduction', *Eight Figurative Painters*, exh. cat. (New Haven: Yale Center for British Art, 1981), 14.

Purchased March 1981
from Knoedler Gallery for £13,800
Oil on wood, 92.7 × 118.1cm
P3968

[**1981**] USA New York, Knoedler Gallery / Federal Republic of Germany Aachen, Neue Galerie–Sammlung Ludwig [**1982**] Federal Republic of Germany Mannheimer Kunstverein / Federal Republic of Germany Kunstverein Braunschweig [**1984**] Italy Venice Biennale / USA Washington, Phillips Collection [**1985**] USA New Haven, Yale Center for British Art / Federal Republic of Germany Hanover, Kestnergesellschaft / England London, Whitechapel Art Gallery [**1987**] England Oxford, Museum of Modern Art / Hungary Budapest, Műcsarnok / Czechoslovakia Prague, Národní Galerie / Poland Warsaw, Zachęta Gallery [**1988**] England Leeds City Art Gallery [**1990**] USSR Kiev, Ukrainian Museum of Fine Art [**1991**] Luxembourg Musée National d'Histoire et d'Art / Bulgaria Sofia, Cyril Methodius Foundation / Argentina Buenos Aires, Museo Nacional de Bellas Artes [**1995**] USA New York, Metropolitan Museum of Art / USA Fort Worth, Modern Art Museum [**1996**] Germany Düsseldorf, Kunstverein für die Rheinlande und Westfalen / England London, Hayward Gallery [**1997**] Italy Rome, British Council [**2002**] Germany Kunstmuseum Wolfsburg [**2003**] France Toulouse, Les Abattoirs / Italy Bologna, British Council [**2005**] Italy Rome, British Council

HOWARD Hodgkin's work, at first, appears daringly simple. Yet those splurges, slicks and virulent marks are the results of a master manipulator, who goads and entreats the paint into doing his bidding. Hodgkin has always sought to represent personal encounters, emotional experiences and memories of the places he has visited. As a young artist he made portraits of friends and fellow artists, and a personal style evolved slowly, becoming, in time, a heat-sealed concentration of image, idea and form. Applied to the conversation pieces he has often painted, talk, setting and personality coalesce and re-emerge in purely pictorial form. Some of Hodgkin's style can be traced to his great love of India, a country he not only knows well, but whose art has influenced his own: his interest in non-Western perspective, for example, which gives equal weight and focus to all parts of the picture; the brightness and density of colour; the border and pattern being on equal terms with the subject-matter. The titles of his works have always alluded to his experiences, whether travelling or being in the company of others, and these make for an intriguing narrative, compelling the viewer to search for clues amid the overlapping abstract planes of colour.

Still Life in a Restaurant was painted while Hodgkin was artist in residence at Brasenose College, Oxford, and it was included in 'Critic's Choice: An Exhibition of Contemporary Art selected by John McEwen' at the ICA in 1978. The painting marks the beginning of a radical transformation in Hodgkin's working method. In 1976, he came across a chemical called Liquin, which reduces the drying time of pigments. It allowed him to build up layers of oil paint without muddying the surface, and as a result his pictures developed a new level of emotional intensity just as the painted surfaces deepened and the density of pigment became more profound. At the same time, Hodgkin virtually eliminated figures from his paintings, clarifying and simplifying his marks so that they appear as no more than dots, stripes, dabs, and the heavy stroke of the brush itself. *Still Life in a Restaurant* is a vibrant work of red, blue and yellow dots hovering over a mottled sea of black, white and grey. It sits, illuminated, inside a heavy dark frame and a thick border of black paint, which Hodgkin explains very simply: 'The more evanescent the emotion I want to convey, the thicker the panel, the heavier the framing, the more elaborate the border, so that this delicate thing will remain protected and intact.'[1] This early work foreshadows Hodgkin's magnificent mural commissioned for the British Council's New Delhi headquarters in 1993. A fixed frame on an immense scale, Hodgkin's mural covers the entire façade of the building, and features a stylised banyan tree and the shadows cast by its leaves. Made out of small rectangular hand-cut tiles of white Makrana marble, and black, locally-quarried Cudappah stone – a technique often used on Mughal buildings – this formidable work by one of the most acclaimed colourists at work today shows Hodgkin's ability to marry the compositional order of European classical art with the intricacies of Indian art. 'Sometimes when I'm in India,' he has said, 'unlike when I'm anywhere else, there are little glimpses when you see encounters between people – compared with the way we all behave, they behave with the utmost circumspection and so forth. It has obviously influenced my painting a lot come to think of it. Because there are glimpses of encounters and things that are almost offstage which suddenly impinge on you very clearly because of the general tempo of life there. There are sort of passionate moments.'[2] AL

1. Hodgkin quoted in Deepak Ananth, 'Hodgkin's Poetics', in *Howard Hodgkin: Small Paintings 1975–1989*, exh. cat. (London: British Council, 1990), 84.

2. Hodgkin quoted in John McEwen, 'Howard Hodgkin', in *The Proper Study: Contemporary figurative paintings from Britain* (London: British Council, 1984).

Purchased November 1978
from Anthony Reynolds Gallery
for £1,798
Mixed media and slide projection
installation, 250 × 300cm
P3699

[1979] France Musée d'Art Moderne
de la Ville de Paris / Belgium Brussels,
Palais des Beaux-Arts [1980] USA New
York, Guggenheim Museum / USA San
Diego, Museum of Contemporary Art /
USA Savannah, Telfair Academy of Arts
and Sciences / USA Austin, University
of Texas / England London, Royal
Academy of Arts [1981] Italy Bergamo
Arte Contemporanea [1994] Russia
St Petersburg, State Russian Museum
[1995] Russia Moscow, New Tretyakov
Gallery / Czech Republic Prague Castle,
Riding School [1996] Germany Museum
Folkwang Essen / France Calais, Le
Channel, Galerie de l'Ancienne Poste
[1998] South Africa Johannesburg Art
Gallery / South Africa Cape Town, South
African National Gallery / Zimbabwe
National Gallery Bulawayo [1999]
Zimbabwe Harare, National Gallery
of Zimbabwe [2000] Cyprus Nicosia
Municipal Arts Centre / Malta Valletta, St
James Cavalier Centre for Creativity

N a career that has spanned over thirty years, Tim Head has created works in such a variety of media that it is difficult to identify a single characteristic. From early installations in which he layered projected images of objects over the real things, to his current explorations in digital media, it would be possible to describe Head's chameleon-like transformations as mirroring the changing nature of technology – and ecology. But this would be to overlook his experimentation in painting in the early 1990s, just at a time when many were pronouncing the medium's demise. Head is constantly questioning perceptions of the truth. He is concerned with optical phenomena, challenging us to make sense of a world in which there is, arguably, no meaning beyond the surface tension – just a collection of light and shadows. From layering slide projections on top of one another to repeating and reducing familiar motifs, Head manipulates our reading of an object or image. There are also environmental concerns at play. In the early 1980s, he commented on excessive consumption in a series of lurid photographs featuring hundreds of tiny plastic toys and a rich, candy-coloured material floating like scum on a toxic sea. He painted familiar consumer motifs, too, such as the Happy Eater logo, which he repeated and manipulated as a means of exploring ideas of genetic mutation.

Head studied under the visionary Pop artist Richard Hamilton at Newcastle University in the mid 1960s. By the end of the decade he was living in New York and working as an assistant to the sculptor Claes Oldenburg, famed for his enormous public sculptures of everyday objects (lipsticks, hamburgers), often made of soft or floppy fabric which innately mocked the very idea of the noble and immutable public monument. Returning to London in the 1970s, Head began teaching at Goldsmiths College. In 1977, he became artist in residence at Clare Hall in Cambridge, and it was here, the following year, that he made *Still Life*. The installation consists of a photograph of a brick wall against which a variety of objects have been placed, including a chair on which a naked woman sits. The image is then turned upside down and re-projected in negative onto the same wall. The result is an uncanny layering of imagery that leaves the viewer completely disorientated. Reality is made indistinguishable from fiction.   JL

Purchased February 1980
from Lisson Gallery for £4,600
Cornish slate, 239 × 130cm
P3876

[1982] Portugal Lisbon, Fundação
Calouste Gulbenkian [1990] USSR Kiev,
Ukrainian Museum of Fine Art [1991]
Luxembourg Musée National d'Histoire
et d'Art / Bulgaria Sofia, Cyril Methodius
Foundation / Argentina Buenos Aires,
Museo Nacional de Bellas Artes [2005]
Ireland Letterkenny, Glebe House and
Gallery [2008] Bangladesh Dhaka,
Bengal Gallery of Fine Arts / Pakistan
Islamabad, PNCA National Art Gallery
/ Kazakhstan Almaty, State Museum of
Fine Arts

*A footpath is a footpath and it is probably the same in China as in
Scotland. It is just one stone after another.*
Richard Long, 1991[1]

FOR over four decades Richard Long has set about uniting the acts
of walking and sculpture, creating momentary, barely perceptible
interventions in the landscape and recording them with carto-
graphic precision and economy. In 1967, while at St Martin's School
of Art in London, Long made the silently iconic work *A Line Made by
Walking*, which consisted of his walking in a line in a field, and then
recording the flattened grass in a photograph.[2] The line's simplicity
etches itself onto the brain. It is a gesture that is at once minimal, uni-
versal and complex: a temporal instant in which the artist is both absent
and present. It is as if he has walked out of the moment and into the
flux of history, somehow embedded in the photographic record without
being in the picture. Hamish Fulton has said, 'When I see an exhibition of Richard Long's art I savour what I imagine were the decisions,
some ideas even causing me to laugh, in appreciation.'[3] We imagine a
lone figure enigmatically ordering nature into an instant of harmonious
precision. His process is organised and ambulatory, considered but also
meaningless; that is to say, quite simply the sum of its parts.

For Long, the straight line has an 'intellectual beauty', whilst the
sculptures 'directly feed the senses'.[4] Mind and body are simultaneously
satisfied: unity and separation at once achieved. The immediacy of the
stones forces the viewer to seek to place them, to absorb and unravel
their context: how they came to be in the landscape, how they gave the
landscape certain qualities, and then how the semi-shamanistic activities of Long have imbued them with a whole new set of meanings. It
forces the viewer to see the blank white walls of the gallery environment
in which the stones now find themselves as a perfectly evolved reposi-
tory for the appreciation of aesthetic beauty. These walls are unnatural,
and yet wholly fitting, and Long reminds us that it is urban Modernism
that provides the frame from which the beauty of the natural world is
being perceived.

Long brings many histories to moments of alignment: the history of
the land, the history of its inhabitants, the history of art and his own
history at a certain point. His works could be said to traverse a ley line
between Arte Povera and Conceptual art. They have a quiet privacy
which is somewhat removed from the clatter of earth-moving machin-
ery in the assured hands of American Land Artists such as Robert
Smithson or Michael Heizer. By contrast, Long's interventions are
hardly interventions at all. Something is picked up and put back down
again. A straightforward record is made. He walks on.   RP

1. Long in interview with Richard Cork, in
Richard Long: Walking in Circles, exh. cat.
(London: South Bank Centre, 1991), 249.

2. Tate Collection, London.

3. Hamish Fulton, 'Old Muddy', in *Richard
Long* (1991), 243.

4. Long in interview with Richard Cork,
249.

Purchased February 1981
from Anthony d'Offay for £3,105
Mixed media, 242 × 202cm

P3963

[**1982**] Japan Tokyo, Metropolitan Art Gallery / Japan Tochigi Prefectural Museum of Fine Arts / Japan Osaka, National Museum of Modern Art / Japan Fukuoka Art Museum / Japan Sapporo, Hokkaido Museum of Art [**1984**] USA Baltimore Museum of Art / USA Contemporary Arts Museum Houston / USA West Palm Beach, Norton Gallery of Art [**1985**] USA Wisconsin, Milwaukee Art Museum / USA New York, Guggenheim Museum [**1987**] England Oxford, Museum of Modern Art / Hungary Budapest, Műcsarnok / Czechoslovakia Prague, Národní Galerie / Poland Warsaw, Zachęta Gallery [**1990**] USSR Kiev, Ukrainian Museum of Fine Art [**1991**] Luxembourg Musée National d'Histoire et d'Art / Bulgaria Sofia, Cyril Methodius Foundation / Argentina Buenos Aires, Museo Nacional de Bellas Artes [**1992**] Italy Bologna, British Council [**1997**] France Paris, Musée d'Art Moderne de la Ville de Paris / Pakistan / Karachi, Hindu Gymkhana / Pakistan Lahore, The Old Fort [**1998**] South Africa Johannesburg Art Gallery / South Africa Cape Town, South African National Gallery / Zimbabwe National Gallery Bulawayo [**1999**] Zimbabwe Harare, National Gallery of Zimbabwe / France Valenciennes, Musée des Beaux-Arts [**2000**] Cyprus Nicosia Municipal Arts Centre / Malta Valletta, St James Cavalier Centre for Creativity [**2003**] Croatia Zagreb, British Council

THIS is perhaps one of Gilbert & George's starkest pictures, concerned with imagery of a dark, malformed growth, and orbiting notions of death and decay. A black silhouette of a skeletal leafless tree appears on a rich yellow background, seeming to raise a twisted claw to the sky. The featured tree grew in Finsbury Circus in London, and was a gift from the Japanese government as reparation after World War II. A poorly-made plaque on the tree detailed its history, though both tree and plaque were removed shortly after Gilbert & George's picture was made. This, along with several related studies from the same period, contrasts with some of the artists' brasher pictures, which teem with life and activity.

Gilbert & George, partners in life and art, have created a universe in which their entire existence is an artwork. From their very first 'Singing Sculpture' (1969), made whilst still students at St Martin's School of Art, and in which they move in synch and sing along with the Depression-era song 'Underneath the Arches', through to their timeless near-matching tailoring, their entirety is heavily formalised. They are well-known icons of British art, although they have always, to some extent, existed as outsiders – never venturing very far from their long-term residence in Fournier Street, East London, and eating in the same cafe every day at the same time. 'Art is for All,' claim Gilbert & George, and 'Art is Life.' As they explain in their inimitable rhetorical style, the subject matter of art 'must be the human condition: we believe in the human condition as the supreme ideal. Man is the most amazing thing of all and the whole formal side of art – colours and forms – is there only to serve the subject and is of no importance in itself. We hate art for art's sake – we are totally opposed to it.'[1]

Gilbert & George have been chroniclers of modern life for more than 40 years, and huge swathes of life – shocks, shits, crucifixes and hoodies – have met within the confines of their signature grid. The themes that concerned the artists in 1980, however, are governed by the twin poles of religion and despair – a faith in life which is bleak and empty. *Intellectual Depression* is prefigured by a gradual move during the 1970s towards darker themes such as depression, alcohol and madness, and draws on a motif of an earlier picture, *Branch* (1978),[2] in which the austere silhouette of a naked branch appears against a red background above the heads of the artists.

Alongside these thematic developments, however, was the start of a new kind of richness in the artists' palette. Gilbert & George had recently moved away from black and white monochrome images, and had begun to develop a process employing a deep red. The year of *Intellectual Depression*, 1980, was the first that they used the colour yellow, in a related picture, *Waiting*.[3] The depth and richness of these hues, fixed within a dark grid-like structure, creates the impression of stained-glass windows. As Suzanne Pagé has noted, 'Like the artists of the Middle Ages, Gilbert & George create images to initiate and explain.'[4] We might imagine that the message preached in this picture is a type of warning. Many pictures from 1980 concern the aesthetics of living with fear, and the use of yellow and black is almost sickly, recalling a hazard sign or a wasp. For such prescient artists, who prefigured an age in which terror would have such an inflated currency, this early picture barks a lesson at us about the effect of strangulation that any such climate of fear has on the intellect, and on the soul. LMF

1. Gilbert & George in interview with Irmeline Lebeer, *Art Press*, 47 (April 1981), 23–25.

2. Private collection.

3. Private collection.

4. Suzanne Pagé, introduction to *Gilbert & George*, exh. cat. (Paris: Musée d'Art Moderne de la Ville de Paris, 1997), 16.

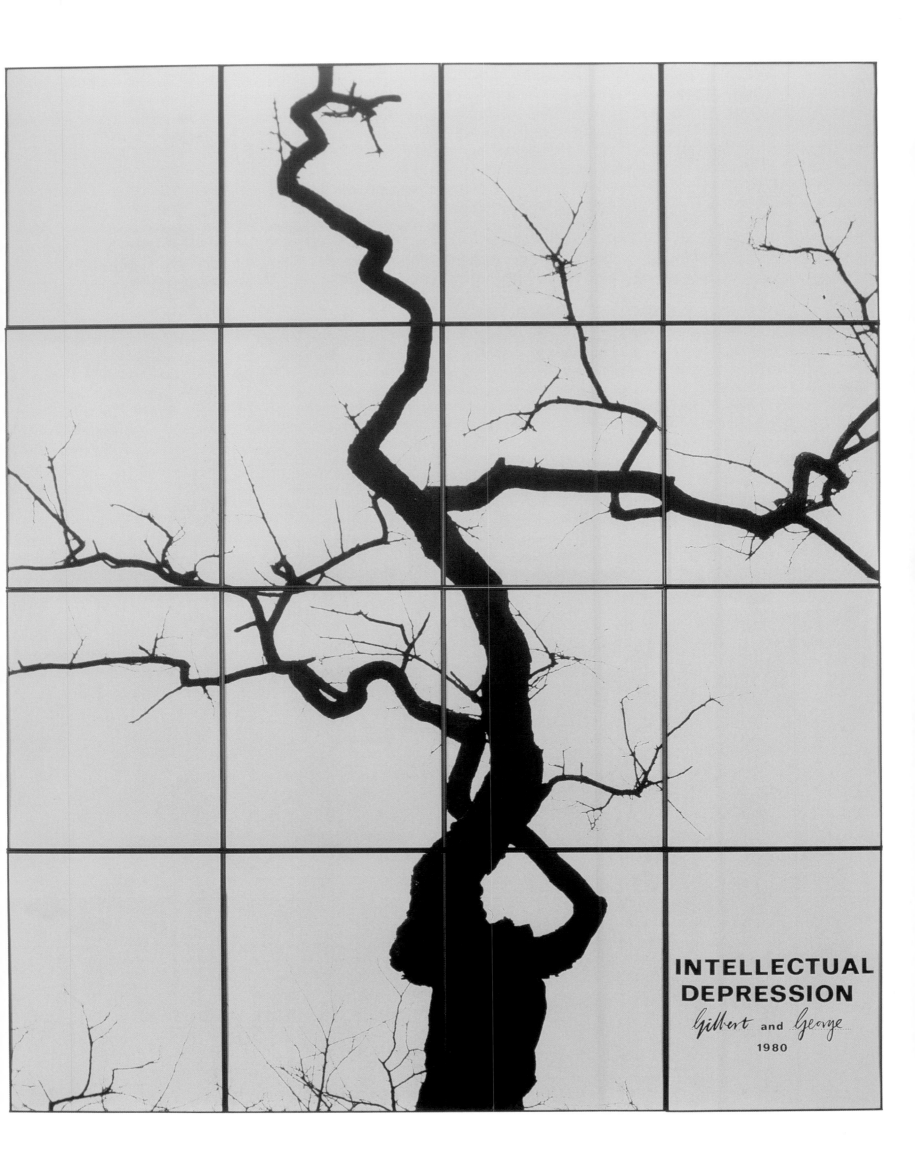

INTELLECTUAL
DEPRESSION
Gilbert and George
1980

Purchased March 1983
from Lisson Gallery for £1,350
Lino and plywood,
91.5 × 183 × 152.2cm
P4276

[1983] Northern Ireland Londonderry, Orchard Gallery / Brazil São Paulo Bienal [1984] Brazil Museu de Arte Moderna do Rio de Janeiro / Mexico Mexico City, Museo de Arte Moderno / Portugal Lisbon, Fundação Calouste Gulbenkian / England London, Tate Gallery / France Villeurbanne, Nouveau Musée / France Aix-en-Provence, Cirva [1985] USA Pittsburgh, Carnegie Museum of Art [1987] Canada Calgary, Alberta College of Art Gallery [1988] USA Long Beach, University Art Museum / Mexico Museo de Arte Contemporáneo de Monterrey / USA Philadelphia, Pennsylvania Academy of Fine Arts [1989] Belgium Antwerp, Museum Van Hedendaagse Kunst / Switzerland Basle, Harry Zellweger Gallery [1990] USSR Kiev, Ukrainian Museum of Fine Art [1991] Luxembourg Musée National d'Histoire et d'Art / Bulgaria Sofia, Cyril Methodius Foundation / Argentina Buenos Aires, Museo Nacional de Bellas Artes [1992] Belgium Brussels, La Borschette [1994] Russia St Petersburg, State Russian Museum [1995] Russia Moscow, New Tretyakov Gallery / Czech Republic Prague Castle, Riding School [1996] Morocco Casablanca, Espace Wafabank / Germany Museum Folkwang Essen / France Paris, Jeu de Paume / France Calais, Le Channel, Galerie de l'Ancienne Poste [1997] Pakistan Karachi, Hindu

S ON of an RAF career pilot, Deacon's work has often been compared to machine parts or the skeletal frames of gliders, hangars or other paraphernalia associated with aviation. In the early 1980s, he began making sculpture which employed swelling, curvilinear forms made from laminated wood, galvanised steel, corrugated iron, cloth and linoleum: materials which were serviceable, readily to hand and not burdened with the weight of sculptural tradition or preconceptions. He has described himself as a fabricator ('material and manipulation are core ideas in what I do'[1]), explaining that he neither carves nor models his materials, but constructs them. The steel rivets, bolts and rough surfaces become part of the final form, reinforcing a sense of the material being manipulated into shape. Despite their debt to industrial processes, the results are surprisingly organic-looking, with, typically, undulating forms that snake into themselves like giant pencil shavings or a DNA double helix. In addition to works of a domestic scale, such as *Boys and Girls (come out to play)*, Deacon has also undertaken a large number of public commissions, many of them inspired by the landscape. The large sculpture *Individual* (2004),[2] for example, began with an aerial photograph he took of the River Tay in Scotland, twisting like a tapeworm through the countryside. Other works begin as doodles on paper and appear to grow like vapour trails, the artist attempting to keep them constantly in a state of transition and flux, full of potential that is never fixed or pinned down.

A prolific writer, Deacon compares sculpture to the spoken word and considers the space in, around and between a sculpture similar to a conversation, with its own rhythms, metaphors and cadences. 'I think of making things, structuring, as being an activity not unlike the power of speech, in that it is a means of giving shape … its obviously not in the same order as language, but it's a means whereby the world, a chaotic universe, is actually made understandable.'[3] He also plays a subversive game with scale, often titling his works using puns, proverbs and nursery rhymes, creating a surprising intimacy between the sculpture and the viewer. Deacon has spoken of Sigmund Freud's theories of play, as outlined in *Beyond the Pleasure Principle* (1920), in which Freud claims that imitative play is a means of mastering the environment around us. Deacon's playfulness in scale, structure and fabrication is brought out in full in a work such as *Boys and Girls (come out to play)*, which was partly inspired by the birth of his daughter. It is made of plywood and wrapped in functional patterned lino featuring a durable Modernist design in yellow, orange and brown. The sculpture resembles a group of discarded and broken spinning tops on the gallery floor, abandoned for more lively pleasures.

A later work by Deacon in the British Council Collection, *Allsorts* (2003), is a reprise on the theme of interlocking circles, a witty cat's cradle in shocking pink. With its interlacing of high-fired ceramic coils, *Allsorts* sits on the floor like a bright new totem, shot through with holes, and reaching for the skies. JL

Gymkhana / Pakistan Lahore, The Old Fort [1998] South Africa Johannesburg Art Gallery / South Africa Cape Town, South African National Gallery / Zimbabwe National Gallery Bulawayo [1999] Zimbabwe Harare, National Gallery of Zimbabwe [2000] Cyprus Nicosia Municipal Arts Centre / Malta Valletta, St James Cavalier Centre for Creativity [2001] Taiwan Taipei Fine Arts Museum [2002] Germany Kunstmuseum Wolfsburg [2003] France Toulouse, Les Abattoirs [2004] Iran Tehran, Museum of Contemporary Art / Romania Bucharest, National Museum of Art [2005] Germany Künzelsau, Museum Würth

1. Quoted in *Turning Points: 20th Century British Sculpture* (Tehran: Tehran Museum of Contemporary Art, 2004), 48.

2. Marion Goodman Gallery, New York.

3. Quoted in *Turning Points*, 48.

Purchased March 1983 from
Lisson Gallery for £3,000
Mixed media, length 800cm

P4278

[**1983**] Italy Museo Civico d'Arte
Contemporanea di Gibellina / **Brazil**
São Paulo Bienal [**1984**] Brazil Museu
de Arte Moderna do Rio de Janeiro /
Mexico Mexico City, Museo de Arte
Moderno / **Portugal** Lisbon, Fundação
Calouste Gulbenkian [**1990**] USSR Kiev,
Ukrainian Museum of Fine Art [**1991**]
Luxembourg Musée National d'Histoire
et d'Art / **Bulgaria** Sofia, Cyril Methodius
Foundation / **Argentina** Buenos Aires,
Museo Nacional de Bellas Artes [**1992**]
Belgium Brussels, La Borschette [**1994**]
Russia St Petersburg, State Russian
Museum [**1995**] Russia Moscow, New
Tretyakov Gallery / **Czech Republic**
Prague Castle, Riding School [**1996**]
Morocco Casablanca, Espace Wafabank
/ **Germany** Museum Folkwang Essen /
France Calais, Le Channel, Galerie de
l'Ancienne Post [**1997**] Pakistan Karachi,
Hindu Gymkhana / **Pakistan** Lahore,
The Old Fort [**1998**] South Africa
Johannesburg Art Gallery / **South Africa**
Cape Town, South African National
Gallery / **Zimbabwe** National Gallery
Bulawayo [**1999**] Zimbabwe Harare,
National Gallery of Zimbabwe / **France**
Valenciennes, Musée des Beaux-Arts
[**2000**] Cyprus Nicosia Municipal Arts
Centre / **Malta** Valletta, St James Cavalier
Centre for Creativity [**2001**] Taiwan
Taipei Fine Arts Museum [**2007**] Italy
Verona, Palazzo della Ragione

TONY Cragg's brief career as a lab technician at the National Rubber Producers Research Association in the late 1960s has often been cited as an indication of the artist-to-be's fascination with synthetic materials. In fact the laboratory did have an impact on Cragg: he was so bored by it that he began to draw to pass the time, and as a result enrolled at Cheltenham School of Art in 1969. Early works were sculptural assemblages created from rubbish and other detritus. Later the rubber factory's influence re-emerges in Cragg's work with Kevlar and polystyrene, which he layered, sandblasted and punctured until they became something else, something alien without past or discernible future. Under his hands, mass-produced materials become sensual objects.

It was in the early 1950s that questions about the environment began to surface as a subject of serious public concern. Cragg was part of the first post-war generation drawn into the debate, and his search for new materials – often ones that could be recycled – led him to invent wholly new forms. His early works in plastic established a vocabulary of materials, objects and images, using the floor and the wall as key elements of the grammar. His innovative use of urban and industrial waste was handled with an invention that opened up a new territory for a generation of sculptors, and which Cragg himself has called 'the new nature'. They dealt with environmental and other social issues in post-industrial Britain with verve and aplomb, and Cragg articulated the developing concern for the natural world using a witty array of scientific-looking objects – flasks, retorts, bottles, hinges, astrolobes and telescopes – and in a dazzling range of materials, from pumice to sandblasted porcelain. Cragg's position as the leading figure in 'The New Sculpture' was confirmed at his solo exhibition held at the Whitechapel Art Gallery in 1981. In 1988, he represented Britain at the Venice Biennale, and won the Turner Prize the same year.

Canoe marks out the basic shape of the ancient watercraft, assembled from broken and discarded pieces of plastic. It opens up a cyclical dialogue between material, object and image. The objects (battered cans, plastic bottles, toy trucks, laundry baskets, sink tidies) are Cragg's sculptural materials, but they remain what they are while at the same time standing in as something else, the building blocks for a new image altogether. On an environmental level, it pictures the island nation drowning in trash of its own making, a harbinger of the plastic tidelines found on every beach and shoreline around the world. On a material level, it works its alchemical magic by translating the broken bits of plastic into a formal artistic organisation, with the unnatural and synthetic greens shading delicately into neutral, then yellow, then red. A year earlier, Cragg had made one of his best-known works, *Britain Seen from the North* (1981),[1] also made of various plastic bits and pieces but mounted on the wall and showing a lone figure viewing an upturned map of Britain. The political comment in both these works can hardly be avoided – a comment on the deregulation and expansionism of the new Thatcher government; and with it all the rejection of older, more stable ideals.   JL

1. Tate Collection, London.

Purchased March 1983
from Lisson Gallery for £2,250
Metal and mixed media,
180 × 190cm

P4277

[**1983**] **England** Oxford, Museum of
Modern Art / **Brazil** São Paulo Bienal
[**1984**] **Brazil** Museu de Arte Moderna
do Rio de Janeiro / **Mexico** Mexico City,
Museo de Arte Moderno / **Portugal**
Lisbon, Fundação Calouste Gulbenkian
[**1985–86**] **Canada** University of Regina,
Norman MacKenzie Art Gallery /
Canada Vancouver Art Gallery / **Canada**
Calgary, Glenbow Museum [**1986**]
Canada Winnipeg Art Gallery / **Canada**
Musée d'Art Contemporain de Montréal
[**1988**] **England** Stoke-on-Trent, City
Museum and Art Gallery [**1990**] **USSR**
Kiev, Ukrainian Museum of Fine Art
[**1991**] **Luxembourg** Musée National
d'Histoire et d'Art / **Bulgaria** Sofia, Cyril
Methodius Foundation / **Argentina**
Buenos Aires, Museo Nacional de Bellas
Artes [**1992**] **Belgium** Brussels, La
Borschette [**1994**] **Russia** St Petersburg,
State Russian Museum [**1995**] **Russia**
Moscow, New Tretyakov Gallery /
Czech Republic Prague Castle, Riding
School [**1996**] **Morocco** Casablanca,
Espace Wafabank / **Germany** / Museum
Folkwang Essen [**1997**] **Pakistan** /
Karachi, Hindu Gymkhana / **Pakistan**
Lahore, The Old Fort [**1998**] **South Africa**
Johannesburg Art Gallery / **South Africa**
Cape Town, South African National
Gallery / **Zimbabwe** National Gallery
Bulawayo [**1999**] **Zimbabwe** Harare,
National Gallery of Zimbabwe / **France**
/ Valenciennes, Musée des Beaux-Arts
[**2000**] **Cyprus** Nicosia Municipal
Arts Centre / **Malta** Valletta, St James
Cavalier Centre for Creativity [**2001**]
Ireland Letterkenny Arts Centre [**2008**]
Bangladesh Dhaka, Bengal Gallery of Fine
Arts / **Pakistan** Islamabad, PNCA National
Art Gallery / **Kazakhstan** Almaty, State
Museum of Fine Arts

T HE sculptures of Bill Woodrow set about enacting feats of metamorphosis, turning everyday objects into new and highly inventive
creations. Woodrow, together with other artists whose work came
to be loosely associated under the title 'The New Sculpture' (among
them Richard Deacon and Tony Cragg), broke away from the austerity
and reductive abstraction that characterised much of the conceptual
work of the 1970s. The Lisson Gallery was to become a staging ground
whereupon they could set about unleashing a flamboyance that was, in
the words of Richard Cork, 'revelling in showmanship, exotic flourishes
and outrageous humour', and at the same time 'boisterous enough
to inaugurate an expansive new mood among young practitioners'.[1]
Discovering a freedom to explore the representational qualities of various found objects and materials, their work had a sense of wit, play and
imagination that held itself up directly to certain aspects of contemporary malaise within society.

In 1981, Woodrow showed the work *Crow and Carrion* (1981),[2] comprising a pair of black umbrellas. The first is broken and crumpled, with
a section of its fabric cut out in the shape of an arm, so that it appears
in two dimensions, almost like a shadow. The second umbrella has
been fashioned into a crow, which is pecking at the exposed limb. *Crow
and Carrion* exhibits the interplay between victim and aggressor that
Woodrow frequently establishes in his works. The umbrellas also highlight the legacy of Surrealism, and Freud's ideas on the uncanny and
the de-familiarisation of the familiar.[3] Woodrow's sculpture is, however,
firmly rooted in the present, utilising the spat-out remnants of a country in the grip of recession, redundancy, anger and waste – all themes
pertinent today.

Long Distance Information, like *Crow and Carrion*, also raises questions that are as relevant now as they were when first made. We can see
that a car bonnet has been cut out to create a pair of walkie-talkies, a
long-lens camera and a bullet, evoking a climate of fear and surveillance,
perhaps exacerbated by the Falklands War of 1982 and its long-range
portrayal by the media back in the UK. Seen from the present day, the
yellow of the bonnet adds a new connotation: the deserts of Afghanistan
and Iraq. It is like trench art on the home front of consumerism.
Nonetheless, this work is by no means neatly polemical – it is imagina-
tive, with a spirit of deviant inversion, resuscitating the old, tired and
discarded, and injecting it with zest and humour. The bonnet forms a
makeshift canvas, whose coarse incisions could almost be hacked-out
plans for a Bauhaus housing scheme. Woodrow himself has said that
this work was inspired by the Chuck Berry hit about striving for com-
munication, 'Memphis Tennessee' (1958):

> *Long distance information, give me Memphis Tennessee*
> *Help me find the party trying to get in touch with me*
> *She could not leave her number, but I know who placed the call*
> *'Cause my uncle took the message and he wrote it on the wall*

RP

1. Richard Cork, *New Spirit, New
Sculpture, New Money: Art in the 1980s*
(London: Yale University Press, 2003), 9.

2. Arts Council Collection.

3. Andrew Causey, 'The New British
Sculpture of the 1980s', in *Blast to
Freeze: British Art in the 20th Century*
(Ostfildern: Hatje Cantz, 2002), 289.

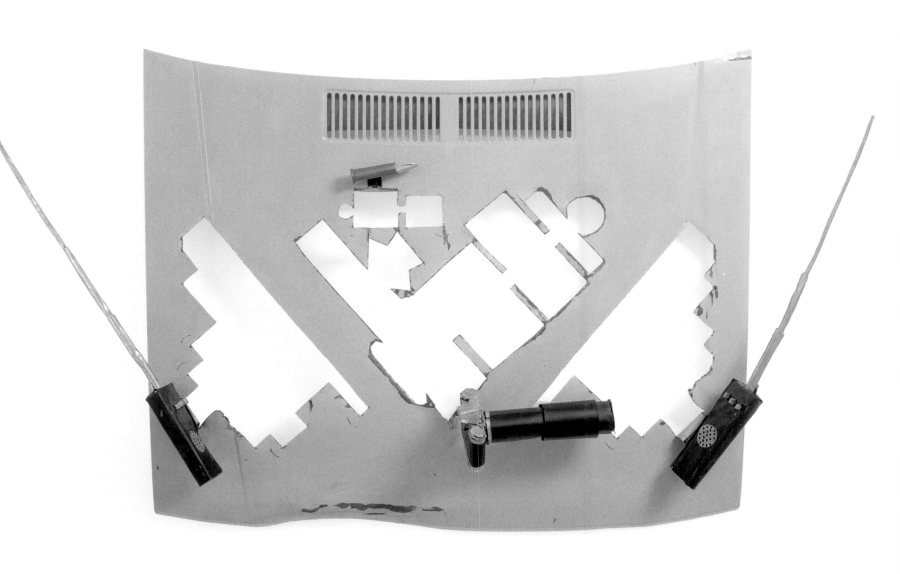

Anish Kapoor
The Chant of Blue, 1983

Purchased July 1983
from Lisson Gallery for £3,000
Polystyrene, resin, gesso and
pigment in four parts, three
pieces 61 × 61 × 61cm, one piece
76 × 76 × 76cm
P4362

[**1983**] Brazil São Paulo Bienal [**1984**]
Brazil Museu de Arte Moderna do Rio
de Janeiro / **Mexico** Mexico City, Museo
de Arte Moderno / **Portugal** Lisbon,
Fundação Calouste Gulbenkian [**1990**]
USSR Kiev, Ukrainian Museum of Fine
Art / [**1991**] Luxembourg Musée National
d'Histoire et d'Art / **Bulgaria** Sofia, Cyril
Methodius Foundation / **Argentina**
Buenos Aires, Museo Nacional de Bellas
Artes [**1992**] Belgium Brussels, La
Borschette [**1994**] Russia St Petersburg,
State Russian Museum [**1995**] Russia
Moscow, New Tretyakov Gallery / **Czech
Republic** Prague Castle, Riding School
[**1996**] Morocco Casablanca, Espace
Wafabank / **Germany** Museum Folkwang
Essen [**1997**] Pakistan Karachi, Hindu
Gymkhana / **Pakistan** Lahore, The Old
Fort [**1998**] South Africa Johannesburg
Art Gallery / **South Africa** Cape Town,
South African National Gallery /
Zimbabwe National Gallery Bulawayo
[**1999**] Zimbabwe Harare, National
Gallery of Zimbabwe [**2000**] Cyprus
Nicosia Municipal Arts Centre / **Malta**
Valletta, St James Cavalier Centre for
Creativity [**2001**] Taiwan Taipei Fine Arts
Museum [**2004**] Iran Tehran, Museum of
Contemporary Art / **Ireland** Letterkenny
Arts Centre

1. Collection of Du Pont Museum of
Contemporary Art, Tilburg.

2. Kapoor in interview with John Tusa
for BBC Radio 3. <http://www.bbc.
co.uk/radio3/johntusainterview/kapoor_
transcript.shtml> accessed February 2009.

ANISH Kapoor's sculptures may be hewn from blocks of stone or made of polished steel, yet he can make shallow depressions look like bottomless pits, and holes look like solid surfaces. In 1992, when he exhibited *Descent into Limbo* (1992)[1] at Documenta in Kassel, audiences were confronted by a deep black hole that looked like a circle of carpet. The power of Kapoor's sculptures lies in our uncertainty as to the boundaries between air and matter, solid and void, tapping into a primal fear of the unknown.

Kapoor's use of pigment in his early sculptures distorts the contours of the shapes he is creating. From deep crimson to cobalt blue, his intense and velvety colours appear to suck up the light around them. Kapoor first began using powdered pigment in his sculptures in 1979, a clear reference to the ritual performances of the Holi Festival in his native India. The earliest examples consisted of formal groupings of chalk and colour. By the time he made *The Chant of Blue*, in 1983, Kapoor was layering the pigment onto polystyrene or fibreglass shapes that looked like strange mineral or plant forms. They were otherworldly, like meteorites or specimens brought back from some distant world, and so alien that they seemed symbolic of a great mystery. Kapoor has said that artists don't make objects, they make mythologies, and that when we look at a work of art we are seeing the mythological context in which the artist is working.[2] Kapoor's context includes great Minimalist sculptors such as Donald Judd and Carl Andre, whom he discovered while studying at Hornsey College of Art and Chelsea School of Art in the 1970s. What had excited him, and what endures in his sculptures, is the Minimalist concept that an object has a language of its own, unconstrained by the history of the maker or the viewer's interpretation. The result is a form that appears to contain the secrets of the universe. JL

Purchased October 1984
from Riverside Studios for £7,090
Lead, fibreglass and clay,
130 × 120 × 90cm
P4961

[**1986**] USA New Haven, Yale Center
for British Art [**1997**] **Pakistan** Karachi,
Hindu Gymkhana / **Pakistan** Lahore,
The Old Fort [**1998**] **South Africa**
Johannesburg Art Gallery / **South Africa**
Cape Town, South African National
Gallery / **Zimbabwe** National Gallery
Bulawayo [**1999**] **Zimbabwe** Harare,
National Gallery of Zimbabwe / **France**
Valenciennes, Musée des Beaux-Arts
[**2000**] **Cyprus** Nicosia Municipal Arts
Centre / **Malta** Valletta, St James Cavalier
Centre for Creativity [**2001**] **Taiwan**
Taipei Fine Arts Museum [**2002**] **England**
Croydon Clocktower [**2004**] **England**
London, BBC / **Romania** Bucharest,
National Museum of Art

CREATOR of innumerable humanoids and an angel so monumental it has transformed the landscape of Gateshead, for the past thirty years Antony Gormley has been using his own body as a template. Casting it in clay, lead and bronze, the result is a collection of mute, self-contained figures with an unnerving presence. Having studied anthropology at Cambridge then Buddhism in India, Gormley's chief concern is with the human psyche, and its relationship with the outside world. His sculptures are invariably situated in public places, watching humanity's struggle with a cold, totemic indifference. It is for this reason he is often described as a public artist, yet he rejects the distinction between 'art' and 'public art', arguing that all art 'desires and demands to be seen'.[1]

Out of this World is an early clay and lead sculpture. Gormley has discussed how unpleasant it can be to work with lead – a nasty, noxious substance. Yet his appreciation of this metal is partly autobiographical. Born in 1950, Gormley grew up during the precarious political climate of the Cold War. From the 1960s to the early 1980s there was a pervasive belief that the world would end in a nuclear holocaust. Many of Gormley's early sculptures were informed by this conviction, and his choice of lead was inspired by the material's ability to insulate against radiation. *Out of this World* consists of a clay figure crouching on top of a large head made from lead. The head is hollowed out, like a shelter, and Gormley has indicated that this could be a protective case for the figure above. The grid across the face could also represent the lines on a globe, suggesting that this is an existential experience in which the seated figure is cowed by the vast, untrammelled cosmos in which it is suspended. The head is also reminiscent of Constantin Brancusi's *Sleeping Muse* (1909–10),[2] an icon of Modernism and one of the components of a group of sculptures that culminated in a simple ovoid called *The Beginning of the World* (1920).[3] Gormley's version could be interpreted as its apocalyptic opposite.   JL

1. Gormley in interview with John Tusa
for BBC Radio 3. <http://www.bbc.co.uk/
radio3/johntusainterview/gormley_
transcript.shtml> accessed February 2009.

2. Hirshhorn Museum and Sculpture
Garden, Washington, DC.

3. Dallas Museum of Art.

Purchased April 1991 from
Karsten Schubert for £8,100
Plaster, 214.6 × 152.4 × 40.6cm
P5919

[**1991**] Germany Berlin, Martin-
Gropius-Bau [**1992**] Belgium Brussels,
La Borschette [**1995**] Poland Łódź,
Muzeum Sztuki [**1997**] Pakistan Karachi,
Hindu Gymkhana / Pakistan Lahore,
The Old Fort [**1998**] South Africa
Johannesburg Art Gallery / South Africa
Cape Town, South African National
Gallery / Zimbabwe National Gallery
Bulawayo [**1999**] Zimbabwe Harare,
National Gallery of Zimbabwe / France
Valenciennes, Musée des Beaux-Arts
[**2000**] Cyprus Nicosia Municipal
Arts Centre / Malta Valletta, St James
Cavalier Centre for Creativity [**2001**]
Taiwan Taipei Fine Arts Museum [**2002**]
Germany Kunstmuseum Wolfsburg
[**2003**] France Toulouse, Les Abbatoirs /
England Cambridge, Jesus College / Brazil
Museu de Arte Moderna do Rio de Janeiro
[**2004**] Brazil Museu de Arte Moderna de
São Paulo

ACHEL Whiteread tends to the overlooked: 'I wanted to give
certain spaces an authority they'd never had.'[1] *False Door* is free-
standing, it commands our sympathy. A workaday door, extracted
from its supporting walls, has been made to stand up for itself. The
rear, a bald façade in six blocks, could pass for an upright Carl Andre.
Conversely, the other side of a foot of plaster is a negative impression
of the door, a rather homely conjunction of two halves. Whiteread
practises a kind of reverse archaeology: filling in to find out. Usually
a mould is negative, but she has cast a positive thing, so the recessed
panels become protrusions and the handle fixture becomes a cavity.
The hole where the handle should be provides spooky punctuation: the
handle is not for turning. Whiteread also drilled holes in a cast of a bath
from the same year, its taps leaving orange rusty marks in the plaster.
She explains that she wanted to create 'an airflow like nostrils. I felt that
it was too claustrophobic, like suggesting my own death.'[2] In the case of
False Door, the hole does *not* pierce all the way through, reinforcing the
sense of claustrophobia. It is a one-way view, as if from inside the body
of the door, invoking the ancient Egyptian belief that dead Pharaohs
would exit their tombs via false doors painted or carved on the inside of
the sarcophagus.[3]

Whiteread uses the chalky inertness of plaster, connoting broken
bones and death masks, to take on the weight of the *vanitas* tradition.
Resolutely monochrome, it rescues the door from the obscurity of
everyday life, fixing its minute textural variations as they are at a
particular moment in time. It is a blockade of detail, discreetly forth-
coming, from smooth, pocked and scumbled patches, to wrinkles in
the lips of the panels, chipped corners and splintery grazes. Tellingly,
Whiteread studied painting at Brighton Polytechnic (1982–85) before
her MA in sculpture at the Slade. David Batchelor distinguishes
Whiteread's 'direct, clear and literal' work from contemporary sculpture
because it 'leaves a sense of something being held back', because this is
'slow sculpture'.[4]

False Door is a clue to bigger projects *Ghost* (1990)[5] and most
famously *House* (1993),[6] which won Whiteread the Turner Prize,
cementing her place on the international stage. (She would go on to win
the Premio Duemila at the XLVII Venice Biennale in 1997.) She took
her own cue, however, from Bruce Nauman's *A Cast of the Space under
my Chair* (1965–68).[7] Where Nauman ribs the weighty seriousness
of Minimalism by insinuating context and allusion, Whiteread makes
context and allusion her essentials. Patrick Elliott remarks, 'Instead of
being abstract and emotionally aloof, Whiteread's work is grounded
in the faithful description – copying even – of specific objects, and
through this implies some sort of narrative.'[8] The concrete yields an
alluring mixture of narratives. Besides the sepulchral, *False Door* is
loaded with a heritage of fictional escapades. It summons up the secret
panelling in a 'Famous Five' adventure, or the other worlds promised
in *The Chronicles of Narnia* or *The Secret Garden*, where doorways are
rites of passage, the thresholds to grown-up life, through which there is
no return.   DF

1. Whiteread in conversation with Iwona
Blazwick, in *Rachel Whiteread*, exh. cat.
(Eindhoven: Stedelijk Van Abbemuseum,
1992), 11.

2. Ibid., 12.

3. Charlotte Mullins, *Rachel Whiteread*
(London: Tate, 2004), 120.

4. David Batchelor, *Rachel Whiteread:
Plaster Sculptures*, exh. cat. (New York:
Luhring Augustine, 1993), 5.

5. National Gallery of Art, Washington,
DC.

6. Commissioned by Artangel Trust and
Beck's, and destroyed in 1994.

7. Visser, Geertjan, Retie, Belgium.

8. Patrick Elliott, 'Sculpting Nothing', in
Rachel Whiteread, exh. cat. (Edinburgh:
National Galleries of Scotland, 2001), 12.

Purchased February 1991 from
Serpentine Gallery for £2,700
Oil on canvas, 200.1 × 240.3cm
P5866

[1992] Belgium Brussels, La Borschette
[1993] Luxembourg Musée National
d'Histoire et d'Art / Turkey Istanbul,
Taksim Art Gallery / Turkey Ankara,
State Fine Art Gallery / Turkey Izmir,
Izfas Gallery [1994] Spain Barcelona,
Centre de Art Santa Monica / Spain
Museo de Bellas Artes de Bilbao / Spain
Madrid, Centro Cultural Galileo / Spain
Murcia, Sala de Exposiciones Verónicas /
Spain Jerez, Sala Pescadería Vieja [1995]
Germany Magdeburg, Kulturhistorisches
Museum [1996] Romania Bucharest,
National Theatre Galleries / Greece
Art Halls of the Cultural Centre of
the Municipality of Athens / Greece
Thessaloniki, Cultural Centre for the
National Bank / Russia St Petersburg,
State Russian Museum / Russia Nizhny
Novgorod, Kremlin Museum / Slovakia
Bratislava, Mirbachov Palace / Czech
Republic Prague, Czech Museum of Fine
Arts, House of the Black Madonna [1997]
Macedonia Skopje, Museum of Modern
Art [1998] Russia St Petersburg, British
Council [2000] Germany ACC Galerie
Weimar / Russia Moscow, Central House
of Artists / Russia St Petersburg, Peter
and Paul Fortress / Italy Rome, Galleria
Nazionale d'Arte Moderna [2001] Spain
Madrid, Centro Cultural Conde Duque
/ France Paris, Espace Elektra / Bulgaria
Sofia, City Art Gallery / Brazil Museu de
Arte Moderna do Rio de Janeiro / Brazil
São Paulo, Instituto Tomie Ohtake / Brazil
Curitiba, Casa Andrade Muricy [2002]
Belgium Le Botanique, Centre Culturel
de la Communauté Wallonie–Bruxelles
/ Slovenia Ljubljana, Moderna Galerija
[2003] South Africa Johannesburg,
British Council

IN 1990, Peter Doig had just finished an MA at Chelsea School of Art and as a winner of the Whitechapel Artists Award was on the cusp of recognition. He was producing paintings that beat a path away from the mainstream: 'In the late 1980s and early 1990s most art had a clean, contemporary, slick look … I purposely made works that were hand-made and homely looking.'[1] Distinctive Doig territory is staked out in *Hill Houses*, a frosty mirage that whiffs of narrative and memory, beckoning beyond the unframed canvas to something as un-contemporary as Monet's *Water Lilies*.

This is a picture whose scattered focus and jumps in perspective result in what Richard Shiff identifies as a 'sensation of roaming.'[2] Through the mistiness, the view takes us by surprise, as if swooping into the windscreen of a car as it races over the skyline. The road, a big vertical stripe, ought to guide us into the scene, but instead forefronts the flatness of the picture plane. Telegraph poles are blurry, not so much pacing out the landscape as shimmying across it. Only in the top third is distance suggested – pinprick windows, a tail-flick of road. It is a meeting ground for the sublime and the kitsch, where sentimental markers, those marzipan houses and fairytale pines, effectively strike a match against the terror of the wilderness.

Doig's story is one of returns. Born in Edinburgh in 1959, his family spent a couple of years in Trinidad before settling in Canada; Doig moved back to Britain, to study at St Martin's School of Art, thereafter returning to Canada (he had a stint as scene painter for film sets in Montreal); it was back to London for his MA, and he now lives in Trinidad. Judith Nesbitt remarks, 'His search for his subject has been curiously linked to his periodic geographical displacement, whereby the visual stimulus of his immediate geographic environment becomes released only with distance.'[3] Yet as much as the large-scale canvases are said to evoke the vast Canadian landscape of his youth, Doig screens off obvious subject matter. Reflecting on early works, he insists, 'They weren't paintings of Canada (though some were) but paintings of an idea of something that was maybe folk – bringing a sort of "homeliness" into art.'[4] This idea of homeliness serves to put hundreds of miles between *Hill Houses*, yellow-stained like an ancient tea tray, and that 'clean, contemporary, slick look'. Fantasies of the open road, shivers of fear and longing: this is an image that creeps up on us, a souvenir of grunge (Nirvana's cult album *Nevermind*, 1991, is counted among Doig's collection of cassettes).[5]

A photograph from *National Geographic*, loosely evoking a childhood spot in Quebec, has been isolated as a source, but even so, *Hill Houses* is a painting about painting as much as anything else. Notably, Doig amplifies the superficiality of snow in terms of its optical effect as well as its Christmas card connotations: 'The snow is all the same size, it's not perspectival, it's this notion of the "idea" of snow which I like. It becomes like a screen, making you look through it.'[6] This predilection for the 'idea' of things, and the emphasis on looking *through* the soft, untidy layers of paint, render the picture open to inference, correspondent to Doig's working method. He prefers to keep paintings unfinished for a period of gestation. He has described the need, on starting out, to open pots of paint all over the studio table and floor, and later to leave a painting alone for long stretches, being thought about, waiting to be returned to.[7]   DF

1. 'Kitty Scott in conversation with Peter Doig', in Adrian Searle, Kitty Scott and Catherine Grenier, *Peter Doig* (London: Phaidon, 2007), 16.

2. Richard Shiff, 'Incidents', in *Peter Doig*, exh. cat. (London: Tate, 2008), 33.

3. Judith Nesbitt, 'A Suitable Distance', in *Peter Doig* (2008), 18.

4. 'Keeping it real', Doig interviewed by Karen Wright, *Modern Painters* (March 2006), 68.

5. 'Peter Doig's Record Collection: A project by Matthew Higgs', in *Peter Doig: Blizzard seventy-seven*, exh. cat. (Kiel: Kunsthalle zu Kiel, 1998), 146.

6. 'Peter Doig: Losing Oneself in the Looking', Doig statement to Leo Edelstein, *Flash Art*, 31 (May–June 1998), 86.

7. Doig in conversation with Chris Ofili, in *Peter Doig* (2008), 122.

Purchased November 1994 from
Anthony Wilkinson for £2,000
Acrylic, oil and elephant dung on
canvas with two elephant dung
supports, 182.5 × 122cm
P6289

[**1995**] **England** Manchester, various
venues [**1996**] **Scotland** Edinburgh,
various venues / **Wales** Cardiff, various
venues [**1997**] **Finland** Helsinki, City
Art Museum [**1998**] **Sweden** Stockholm,
Royal Academy of Fine Arts / **Ukraine**
Kiev, Soros Foundation / **Poland** Warsaw,
Zachęta Gallery / **Germany** Chemnitz,
Städtische Kunstsammlungen / **Czech
Republic** Prague, National Gallery
of Modern Art / **Croatia** Zagreb,
Zagreb Union of Croatian Artists
[**1999**] **Germany** Darmstadt, Institut
Mathildenhöhe / **Lithuania** Vilnius,
Contemporary Art Centre / **Hungary**
Budapest, Ludwig Múzeum / **Slovakia**
Bratislava, Slovak National Gallery /
Romania Bucharest, National Theatre
Galleries [**2001**] USA Los Angeles,
Museum of Contemporary Art [**2003**]
England Manchester, British Council
[**2005**] **Nigeria** Lagos, British Council

WITH a rich-patterned surface teeming with earthy glow, *Painting with Shit on it* occupies a somewhat pivotal place in Chris Ofili's early work, allowing him to continue a long-term love affair with painting and, one might suggest, with beauty. The year when it was painted, 1993, was fundamental in the development of Ofili's work and its uneasy integration of black culture, painting, dung, the sacred and the profane and the glistening appeal of decoration; and many of these elements meet in this particular work.

The mythology surrounding this painting is rich and confusing, beginning in the previous year, when Ofili was still a student at the Royal College of Art, London. He took a British Council sponsored trip to Zimbabwe, picking up on both the sacred nature of elephant dung in the country, and also on the excessively rich dot technique used in the cave paintings of the Matopos Hills. On his return, Ofili further explored the connotations of this new material, buying an advert in *Frieze* that featured simply the bold text 'ELEPHANT SHIT', and creating readymade graffiti stickers with the same phrase, which he stuck all over London. Borrowing from American artist David Hammons, who sold snowballs at a market, he even took to displaying (not selling) the dried elephant dung in Brixton. The 'creation myth' of the Zimbabwe trip is widely reported, having been twisted around the mythology of the black artist (Ofili is Manchester-born of Nigerian descent) 'finding' their blackness on a trip to Africa, and Ofili has worked with and against this mythologising, even joking once that the story had been made up.[1]

What Ofili could be said to do at this point, is to start using any black style or reference he might choose. Hip-hop, a huge influence on his work, makes much of the 'sample' and the namecheck, and this is, arguably, the device he adopts with a huge selection of black culture, thus somewhat destabilising those tenets of multiculturalism which had 'created a double bind for artists of colour who benefited from its aims, but were also ghettoised by its narrow compartmentalising of their work, one that did not allow it to be seen in the context of the art of their white peers'.[2]

In *Painting with Shit on it*, the biggest hook, the biggest sample of all, is the elephant dung, which is 'on' the painting, as the title suggests. Yet the painting is also 'on' two little pedestals made of dung, a supporting device which Ofili would continue to use for many years. In later works, such as *The Holy Virgin Mary* (1996)[3] and Ofili's major work, *The Upper Room* (1999–2002),[4] the glazed glossy lumps of dung would be integrated into the resinous, sticky surface of the entire canvas, and covered in glamorous glitter and pins. However, in this work, as Godfrey Worsdale has pointed out, the 'distinction between the painting and the shit was made manifest even in the titling of the work, almost as if the dung took the painting somewhere else without ever becoming an integral element'.[5]

This move also, however, allows beauty back onto the canvas. As Ofili has said, 'The paintings themselves are very delicate abstractions, and I wanted to bring their beauty and decorativeness together with the ugliness of the shit and make them exist in a twilight zone'.[6] The baggage of this borrowing, combined with the sanctioned transgression of shit on canvas, allowed Ofili to create some of the most compellingly resplendent paintings of the late 20th century, defying you not be seduced by their fecund wonder.   LMF

1. Godfrey Worsdale (ed.), *Chris Ofili*, exh. cat. (Southampton: Southampton City Art Gallery, 1998).

2. Lisa G. Corrin, 'Confounding the Stereotype', in *Chris Ofili* (1998), 14.

3. The Saatchi Gallery, London.

4. Tate Collection, London.

5. Godfrey Worsdale, 'The Stereo Type', in *Chris Ofili* (1998), 2.

6. Ofili in interview with Marcelo Spinelli, in *Brilliant! New Art from London*, exh. cat. (Minneapolis: Walker Art Center, 1995), 67.

33

Damien Hirst Apotryptophanae, 1994

Purchased May 1994 from
Serpentine Gallery for £8,500
Household gloss and emulsion
paint on canvas, 205.5 × 221cm
P6271

[1995] Germany Cologne, British Council [1997] Finland Helsinki, City Art Museum [1998] Sweden Stockholm, Royal Academy of Fine Arts / Ukraine Kiev, Soros Foundation / Poland Warsaw, Zachęta Gallery / Germany Chemnitz, Städtische Kunstsammlungen / Czech Republic Prague, National Gallery of Modern Art / Croatia Zagreb, Zagreb Union of Croatian Artists [1999] Germany Darmstadt, Institut Mathildenhöhe / Lithuania Vilnius, Contemporary Art Centre / Hungary Budapest, Ludwig Múzeum / Slovakia Bratislava, Slovak National Gallery / Romania Bucharest, National Theatre Galleries [2000] England London, British Council [2001] Taiwan Taipei Fine Arts Museum / Portugal Lisbon, British Council [2008] Japan Tokyo, Mori Art Museum

IN 1994 Damien Hirst was dicing with institutional sanction, between nomination for the Turner Prize (1993) and winning it (1995). He already occupied a senior position among a generation of young British artists distinctive enough to win the laurels of the definite article. It was a diverse group that blossomed in the late 1980s, many on the fine art course at Goldsmiths, where Michael Craig-Martin and Jon Thompson had replaced specialist divisions with an emphasis on context – art historical, professional, social. Hirst's 'Pharmaceutical Paintings', also known as the spot paintings, began at that time. Two were painted onto the walls of an ex-London Port Authority building at Surrey Docks for 'Freeze', the show that Hirst, then a second-year student, had a much feted part in organising. This was in the wake of Prozac's hugely hyped launch, but it was an ongoing series. 'The infinite possibilities in painting just kill me,' he says, and to this day continues to chase the idea of a 'rainbow in a room'.[1]

A big-time snooker fan, in *Apotryptophanae* Hirst cues up mortal questions across the canvas. The spot paintings, measured rows of dots, emanate from the packaging of pharmaceuticals and are titled alphabetically. Names needn't be genuine (Tryptophan is produced commercially as an anti-depressant; links to a health scare led to an international ban in 1991). Hirst's studio takes a quasi-scientific approach to production, aiming for machine-like detachment and accuracy. Paintings needn't be executed by Hirst (he attributes the best to an assistant, Rachel Howard, another Goldsmiths graduate). Medical colour codes are blown up microscopically, exposing as entirely abstract the promise of respite in the limbo between birth and death. Colours are configured differently on every canvas. This is systematic randomness on an overwhelming scale, yet at the same time, as Hirst admits, 'they're a bit childish – a bit like sweets or smarties, or drugs. I had my stomach pumped as a child because I ate pills thinking they were sweets. So did my brother.'[2] Colour is an abiding narcotic: 'I love colour. I feel it inside me. It gives me a buzz.'[3]

In *Apotryptophanae* the spots, fifteen up and fourteen across, scatter the gaze, like the handfuls of pills thrown over Keith Allen in Hirst's video for 'Country House' (1995), the hit by fellow Goldsmiths graduates, Blur, that was to be an anthem for Britpop. Spots are, of course, a ubiquitous tool in graphic design (the British Council logo, until 2004, was a grey and red Union Jack picked out in a square of seven spots). Yet, thanks to Hirst, the 1990s contracted a peculiar epidemic of candy-coloured measles, from wrapping paper, to adverts for British Airways' low-budget airline Go, to the exterior of the Tate Boat, designed by Hirst himself. In exploiting the juncture between art and popular visual culture, he succeeded in branding an era.

Hirst's idiom, verbal and visual, is one of insouciant contradiction: the spot paintings, he insists, have 'nothing to do with Richter or Poons or Bridget Riley or Albers or even Op. They're about the urge or the need to be a painter above and beyond the object of a painting. I've often said that they are like sculptures of paintings. I started them as an endless series like a sculptural idea of a painter (myself).'[4] *Apotryptophanae* asks to be situated within a dot-to-dot of artistic highs and economic bubbles, a giant, continuous puzzle. Throughout his work, Hirst evinces an almost 17th-century appreciation of the beauty of cataloguing – butterflies, fish, animal carcasses, skeletons, surgical equipment, cancer cells, diamonds. Cataloguing is an interminable process: it negates the point of a final result. 'There's no answers, only questions, and hopefully the questions will help guide you through the darkness.'[5] Nowhere less so than in *Apotryptophanae*, whose polka dots offer a dazzling, vivacious guide to the dance of death. 'I really think they do move, that's why I'll never stop doing them. They won't fucking keep still.'[6] DF

1. Richard Cork, 'Every Story is so Different: Myth and Reality in the YBA/Saatchi Decade', *Young British Art, The Saatchi Decade* (London: Booth-Clibborn, 1999), unpaginated.

2. Damien Hirst, *I Want to Spend the Rest of My Life Everywhere, With Everyone, One to One, Always, Forever, Now.* (London: Booth-Clibborn, 1997), 250.

3. Hirst, 'On Painting Dumb', in *I Want to Spend the Rest of My Life …*, 246.

4. Ibid.

5. Hirst interviewed by Sean O'Hagan, *New Religion*, exh. cat. (London: Paul Stolper / Other Criteria, 2006), 9.

6. Richard Cork, 'Every Story is so Different …', unpaginated.

34

Douglas Gordon 10 ms⁻¹, 1994

Purchased January 1995
from Lisson Gallery for £5,000
Video installation
P6292

[1995] Italy Venice, Scuola di San
Pasquale / England Manchester, various
venues [1996] Scotland Edinburgh,
various venues / Wales Cardiff, various
venues / Israel Jerusalem, Art Focus /
Jerusalem Foundation [1997] Portugal
Lisbon, Fundação Calouste Gulbenkian
/ Finland Helsinki, City Art Museum
[1998] Sweden Stockholm, Royal
Academy of Fine Arts / Ukraine Kiev,
Soros Foundation / Poland Warsaw,
Zachęta Gallery / Germany Chemnitz,
Städtische Kunstsammlungen / Czech
Republic Prague, National Gallery
of Modern Art / Croatia Zagreb,
Zagreb Union of Croatian Artists
[1999] Germany Darmstadt, Institut
Mathildenhöhe / Lithuania Vilnius,
Contemporary Art Centre / Hungary
Budapest, Ludwig Múzeum / Slovakia
Bratislava, Slovak National Gallery /
Romania Bucharest, National Theatre
Galleries [2000] Cyprus Nicosia
Municipal Arts Centre / Malta Valletta,
St James Cavalier Centre for Creativity
[2001] Taiwan Taipei Fine Arts Museum
/ Germany Munich, Kunsthalle der Hypo-
Kulturstiftung / Poland Kraków, Gallery of
Contemporary Art Bunkier Sztuki [2002]
Hungary Budapest, MEO Contemporary
Art Centre / England Eastbourne, Towner
Art Gallery [2004] Romania Bucharest,
National Museum of Art [2006] Thailand
Bangkok, Tonson Gallery / China
Guangzhou, Guangdong Museum of Art
[2007] China Beijing, Capital Museum

T is hard to look away from the painfully slowed-down frames of
blistered silver film in Douglas Gordon's *10 ms⁻¹*. A silent, looped
video projection on a large tilted screen depicts a man, who falls to
the ground in an almost balletic dive, and then appears unable to get
up. His awkward attempts to stand are frustrating and pathetic. The
environment is hard and stark – one can make out what looks to be a
hard bed to the right-hand side. He is wearing only underwear, adding
to his vulnerability; his pale, quite useless limbs appear to thwart him as
he tries different ways of getting to his feet. This work follows *24 Hour
Psycho* (1993),[1] which also employs slow-motion process, and is perhaps
Gordon's best-known work. However, whilst the material appropriated
for that work, Alfred Hitchcock's *Psycho* (1960), is almost archetypal,
part of the reason *10 ms⁻¹* is so effective is because the source footage
is unknown.

The large scale of the projection renders the figure life-sized to
us. The tilting of the screen upsets our own balance somewhat, so we
approach the figure in the footage as an equal, identifying with his sorry
plight. The man is clearly in distress, inviting our pity and sympathy.
Repeated attempts and failures, however, begin to wear on us, and
discomfort provokes us to consider what we are watching. Caught in an
endless cycle of build-up and failure, we separate ourselves from him.
We begin to wonder what is wrong. He looks healthy enough. We might
discover that the found footage dates to the First World War, adding a
new layer of pathos and historical weight to our reading of what we see.
Is the problem, then, psychological? Madness induced by the horrors
of war, or shell-shock? Why is there a camera watching this man in the
first place, and why will no-one assist him? It may occur to us that the
event is staged – a medical document or training video.

Indeed, the objective, fascinated gaze that this film encourages of
us might be termed 'medical'. As Gordon has commented in an interview, 'Fear and repulsion and fascination are critical elements in both
the world of this science [neuropsychology] and the world of cinema.'[2]
Two other specifically analogous works, made by Gordon shortly after,
broached similar themes. *Hysterical* (1994–95)[3] features another very
questionable piece of footage, in which a young woman is provoked into
a fit and then restored, for the benefit of the camera. In another, *Fuzzy
Logic* (1995),[4] we witness the last twitching movements of a dying fly.
What impels us to watch these images, feeling horrified yet strangely
cold and clinical, is the question at the core of these works. In every
one, the subject of the film is a prisoner to the camera, just as we the
viewer are prisoner to the film, locked in a cold embrace. Interestingly,
the more we might emotionally disconnect from what is happening on
screen, the more we are drawn to examine the texture of the antique
footage, and to consider film in and of itself. As Raymond Bellour has
succinctly commented, 'Gordon lends the cinema a voice that could
say: I am dead but I am still alive enough to tell you this.'[5] What this
particular piece of footage might remind us is that there is a quality deeply inherent in the fabric of film, that contains the following
uncomfortable message, and wills us to obey: 'Look. Look. Look.' LMF

1. Private collection and Kunstmuseum
Wolfsburg. Edition of 2.

2. 'Attraction–répulsion', Gordon
interviewed by Stéphanie Moisdon-
Trembley (1996), in Douglas Gordon,
*Déjà-vu: Questions and Answers, Volume
1, 1992–1996* (Paris: Musée d'Art Moderne
de la Ville de Paris, 2000), 110.

3. Southampton City Art Gallery
and Musée Départemental d'Art
Contemporain de Rochechouart. Edition
of 2.

4. Edition of 3.

5. Raymond Bellour, 'The Instant of
Seeing', in *Douglas Gordon*, exh. cat.
(Lisbon: Centro Cultural de Belém, 1999),
27.

Purchased November 1996 from
Anthony Reynolds for £7,500
Video installation on 4 monitors,
with flight cases
P6682

[**1997**] Finland Helsinki, City Art
Museum [**1998**] Sweden Stockholm,
Royal Academy of Fine Arts / Ukraine
Kiev, Soros Foundation / Poland Warsaw,
Zachęta Gallery / Germany Chemnitz,
Städtische Kunstsammlungen / Czech
Republic Prague, National Gallery
of Modern Art / Croatia Zagreb,
Zagreb Union of Croatian Artists
[**1999**] Germany Darmstadt, Institut
Mathildenhöhe / Lithuania Vilnius,
Contemporary Art Centre / Hungary
Budapest, Ludwig Múzeum / Slovakia
Bratislava, Slovak National Gallery /
Romania Bucharest, National Theatre
Galleries [**2001**] England London, Tate
Modern [**2002**] USA Ridgefield, Aldrich
Contemporary Art Museum [**2003**]
Germany Berlin, Akademie der Künste
[**2006**] China Guangzhou, Guangdong
Museum of Art [**2007**] China Beijing,
Capital Museum

CHARACTERISTICALLY deadpan, Mark Wallinger presents a
series of video monitors on top of wheeled flight cases, each
isolating the royal carriage's leisurely progress down the racecourse on the Tuesday, Wednesday, Thursday and Friday (respectively)
of Royal Ascot, red-letter days in the calendar of institutional frivoli-
ties. Simultaneous footage exposes precise choreography: the Queen's
frozen smile and rigid curls, the tilt of her head, her gloved wave, the
Duke of Edinburgh raising his top hat, the national anthem striking up.
Appropriately for an event whose media coverage focuses on the parade
of hats and dresses rather than the sport, here we have a close-up on
clothes, on the Queen's dolly mixture of pinks, tangerines, limes; the
difference from day to day is barely discernible, just as the four BBC
commentaries merge in a confused blather.

This repetition of imagery, all backed by bright green turf, brings into
play Andy Warhol's late screenprints of Elizabeth II from his 'Reigning
Queens' series (1985),[1] a quartet of the postage stamp icon in camp
conjugations of Hollywood make-up and bubblegum colours. In *Royal
Ascot* Wallinger harnesses the aesthetic and pleasures of the racecourse,
a strapping mount for entering into the debate about constitutional
inertia – a debate that had garnered new piquancy (by 1994 the Queen
and Prince Charles were liable for tax, and Buckingham Palace had
opened to the public). Ian Hunt locates *Royal Ascot* within Wallinger's
agenda of 'innocent protest' across different media, as 'a private protest
and analysis of a situation which appears baffling or intolerable rather
than a piece of speech-making'.[2] If Warhol's portrait series implies
that monarchy is an assignment in the eyes of its subjects, in our
effortless recognition of Wallinger's footage, the charms as well as the
absurdity and fatigue of continuity add up to something rather more
subtle. Adding an emotional dimension to the conceptual value of the
racecourse (bound up in class and pedigree), the quadruped was also a
personal passion of Wallinger's. In 1993, he bought a racehorse with a
consortium organised by his dealer, Anthony Reynolds. He named it *A
Real Work of Art*. Although it ran just one race before injury, it won him
a Turner Prize nomination and extended the Duchampian idea of the
readymade into something with feeling.

On completing his MA, Wallinger stayed on at Goldsmiths to teach
(1986–91), and his central position among the rising generation there
saw him included in Saatchi's landmark show 'Young British Artists II'
(1993). Wallinger dared to tickle the touchy underarms of politics; for
this encounter, sport, its traditions and mass appeal, proved to be an
accommodating arena. 'It was a reaction to what was happening in the
eighties when artists seemed to think it was more important to appeal
to rich people in Cologne than to a more general audience.'[3] Glance
at the photograph from the same period, *Mark Wallinger, 31 Hayes
Court, Camberwell New Road, Camberwell, London, England, Great
Britain, Europe, The World, The Solar System, The Galaxy, The Universe*
(1994).[4] The artist and his brother stand amid a crowd of football fans
emerging from Wembley, and hold aloft a Union Jack with 'Wallinger'
written across the middle. They risk a fight by dipping a divining rod
into the currents of hooliganism, fandom and solipsism that flowed
through debates about national identity. And adjoining that debate,
the quadruple monitors of *Royal Ascot* undercut the definitive with
ellipsis.   DF

1. Government Art Collection.

2. Ian Hunt, 'Protesting Innocence', in
Mark Wallinger: Credo, exh. cat. (London:
Tate, 2000), 22.

3. Wallinger quoted by Rose Aidin,
'Profile: Mark Wallinger – Race, class and
sex', *The Independent* (2 June 2001), 5.

4. Anthony Reynolds Gallery, London.

Angus Fairhurst
A Cheap and Ill-Fitting Gorilla Suit, 1995

Purchased December 1996 from Riding House Editions for £960
Colour videotape, 5 mins.
P6700

[1997] Finland Helsinki, City Art Museum [1998] Sweden Stockholm, Royal Academy of Fine Arts / Ukraine Kiev, Soros Foundation / Poland Warsaw, Zachęta Gallery / Germany Chemnitz, Städtische Kunstsammlungen / Czech Republic Prague, National Gallery of Modern Art / Croatia Zagreb, Zagreb Union of Croatian Artists [1999] Germany Darmstadt, Institut Mathildenhöhe / Lithuania Vilnius, Contemporary Art Centre / Hungary Budapest, Ludwig Múzeum / Slovakia Bratislava, Slovak National Gallery / Romania Bucharest, National Theatre Galleries

THE gorilla suit hides within it an implicit sense of a joke, an association inherited from moving-image skits. Like a banana skin on the floor, or the grand piano waiting to be dropped, its appearance signifies comedy, and sets humorous expectations in motion. The comedy of the gorilla suit lies in an attempt to frighten that is somehow failed – the journey from King Kong to his pathetic, almost quaint, imitation.

In Angus Fairhurst's 1995 video, *A Cheap and Ill-Fitting Gorilla Suit*, the artist appears in a room, standing still and dressed in the aforementioned shoddy costume, shiftily appearing to wait for something. He begins heavily jumping, in a kind of gorilla impersonation, stretching the suit's capability for movement as it begins to rip open. Newspaper stuffing falls from the disguise, the suit becomes thin and baggy, and over the next few minutes Fairhurst gradually tears free. Near the end, he seems to tire at the last hurdle, gathering strength before finally breaking out – a vulnerable, naked body hidden within the big scary disguise. He makes two naked victory jumps, before running from the scene – in his own words, 'a skinny lanky geezer'.[1]

A striking feature of this video is how pallid and almost monochromatic the scene is. Were it not for a brown wooden staircase caught in the top left frame, for the most part the video appears almost as black and white as the newspaper that comes tumbling out. It is only when we glimpse some pale peach flesh as the suit rips, that any colour enters the action. The ashen palette is just one indicator of the melancholy that is as much at the heart of Fairhurst's work as the comedy. The idea of the 'ill-fit' crops up in many other works; for example, *When I Woke Up in the Morning the Feeling Was Still There* (1996), a series of screenprints also in the British Council Collection. These feature monochrome photographic images of a man holding up a large square of card on top of which a bright colour has been printed and deliberately mis-registered – conveying a sense that this bright, dream-like pop of emotion cannot fit squarely into the man's colourless life.

The gorilla, too, featured many times in the artist's work, in drawings and cartoon sketches, often as a stand-in for the human figure, but also as a device to demonstrate a confounding of expectations. In Fairhurst's drawings, a gorilla suit would open up to reveal, for example, a little fish inside. In a bronze sculpture, *A Couple of Differences Between Thinking and Feeling II* (2003),[2] a gorilla stares at its arm, which lies severed on the floor. It looks as though it is thinking 'Is that really mine? Is that really me?' Thus the body in Fairhurst's work is represented either as a kind of strong protection for the slippery fragile thing inside, or, more commonly, as a disappointing prison.

It is difficult not to think of the gorilla suit in Fairhurst's comment to his friend Damien Hirst: 'The other day I saw a frail old man get on the Underground, having been hit by time. He must think "how dare time have done this to my body so that I can no longer jump on trains as quickly as my mind does?"'[3] The melancholic fantasy of *A Cheap and Ill-Fitting Gorilla Suit* lies in the idea of breaking free of the confines and restrictions of the body – a denial of the absurd idea that a body represents a soul. The punch line, of course, is that the one can't survive without the other.   LMF

1. Fairhurst in interview with Martin Gayford, *Telegraph Magazine* (28 February 2004).

2. The Saatchi Gallery, London.

3. Fairhurst in interview with Damien Hirst, *Angus Fairhurst*, exh. cat. (Art Studio: Milan, 1992), 23.

Purchased December 1995
from Jay Jopling for £10,000
Nickel-plated brass pins, compass,
canvas and glue, 67 × 112 × 1.5cm
P6488

[1995] Turkey Istanbul Biennial [1997]
Finland Helsinki, City Art Museum
[1998] Sweden Stockholm, Royal
Academy of Fine Arts / Ukraine Kiev,
Soros Foundation / Poland Warsaw,
Zachęta Gallery / Germany Chemnitz,
Städtische Kunstsammlungen / Czech
Republic Prague, National Gallery of
Modern Art / Croatia Zagreb, Union
of Croatian Artists [1999] Germany
Darmstadt, Institut Mathildenhöhe /
Lithuania Vilnius, Contemporary Art
Centre / Hungary Budapest, Ludwig
Múzeum / Slovakia Bratislava, Slovak
National Gallery / Romania Bucharest,
National Theatre Galleries [2004]
Romania Bucharest, National Museum of
Art [2006] USA New York, Museum of
Modern Art [2008] Bangladesh Dhaka,
Bengal Gallery of Fine Arts / Pakistan
Islamabad, PNCA National Art Gallery
/ Kazakhstan Almaty, State Museum of
Fine Arts

THIS work was made as part of a series of carpets that Mona Hatoum produced for the Istanbul Biennial of 1995. Upon first sight, it could have been picked up from the city's Grand Bazaar, but is in fact made from thousands of upturned nickel-plated brass pins glued to a canvas, with a compass placed at its centre to allow orientation towards Mecca. Guy Brett has described how the work should not be seen merely as an ironic satire on religiosity but also as 'a poetic, imagination-stretching invention, that re-circles on itself to evoke the cosmic wonder of a starry sky'.[1] The work feeds into a lineage of radical floor-based activities including those of Jackson Pollock, Carl Andre and Richard Long, as well as Arte Povera artists such as Jannis Kounellis and Piero Manzoni. Hatoum adds her own voice, although the focus of her dialogue is not so much with these male trailblazers as between the materials that she selects and their impact on the viewer's perceptions and emotions.

Hatoum was born in Lebanon to Palestinian parents. She attended Beirut University, studying graphic design, before coming to England in 1975 just as war broke out in her homeland. Forced into exile she enrolled at Byam Shaw School of Art before continuing at the Slade. In a practice that incorporates installation, sculpture, performance, photography and film and video, her work has, from the beginning, been focused on the body as the 'axis of our perceptions' – a site of activism, struggle and persecution.[2] In 1985, she laced up a pair of shiny Doc Martens boots and strode through the streets of Brixton, an area undergoing severe race riots at the time. The boots evoke both vulnerability and authority; they could belong to a skinhead or a policeman. They are powerless yet hauntingly animated. The work combines humour with a nuanced understanding of an object's symbolic qualities and a genuine engagement with the urgency of place.

Whilst in Hatoum's performances her own body is the principle stage upon which meaning is fought out, in her installations and sculpture the key relationship is between object, viewer and space. Her deliberate forms are beautiful but loaded, revealing complexities and contradictions. A tension exists between, on the one hand, a desire for the formal harmony of abstract forms and aesthetic models, and, on the other, a deep suspicion of their potentially de-humanising qualities. The sculptures are imbued not only with the phenomenological language of Minimalism, but also a struggle for political voice in a complex contemporary world. *Prayer Mat* asks us to consider our structures of belief and the means by which we go about private moments of spiritual engagement. It manages to be serious with a light touch; at once sensitive to the individual and also conscious of the systems within which individuals operate.   RP

1. Guy Brett, 'Survey', in Michael Archer, Guy Brett and Catherine de Zegher, *Mona Hatoum* (London: Phaidon, 1997), 77.

2. Hatoum in conversation with Michael Archer, in *Mona Hatoum* (1997), 8.

Mike Nelson
The Black Art Barbecue, San Antonio, August 1961, 1998

Purchased March 2002 from Matt's Gallery for £10,000
A replicant working desk as Alchemist's desk, based on an engraving by Albrecht Dürer entitled *Saint Jerome in his Study*, 1514, mixed media, dimensions variable

P7259

[**2002**] Chile Santiago, Museo Nacional de Bellas Artes [**2003**] Venezuela Caracas, Museo Alejandro Otero / Mexico Mexico City, Museo de Arte Carrillo Gil / Colombia Bogotá, Biblioteca Luis-Angel Arango [**2004**] Panama Panama City, Museo de Arte Contemporáneo / Guatemala Guatemala City, Museo de Arte Moderna / Brazil São Paulo, SESI / Brazil Rio de Janeiro, Museu de Arte Contemporânea de Niterói

ONE might be forgiven for thinking that Mike Nelson's artworks are equally involved in the 'dark arts' of black magic as they are in contemporary art practice. This is more explicit in *The Black Art Barbecue, San Antonio, 1961* than in many works, through the installation's allusion to the art of shrines, totems and voodoo. Like an alchemist, the artist experiments with the splutters and fizz that can be created by combining several elements, but he also plays the part of fraud and trickster.

The Black Art Barbecue is a recreation of an artist's desk in a studio. The title of the work is taken from an amalgamation of the various drawings that are hung over the desk. Like much of Nelson's work, the tableau of objects creates the impression that we have stumbled upon a room that has just been left. In the case of *The Black Art Barbecue*, it appears that before leaving, the (fictional) artist was closely examining a book with a magnifying glass. On the desk are a pair of effigies roughly hewn from green packing foam: a tiny couple – male and female. Surrounding the little figures' feet are twigs, representing, one must presume, firewood for a bonfire. Flames made from red plastic seem to lick at their bodies, as though they are martyrs burned at the stake or, perhaps more likely, a pair of voodoo dolls. Around the desk is a strange assortment of work tools, totems and keepsakes, including more twigs, animal skulls, paper stars that seem to have been stencilled on the desk, and plastic cases for reels of film.

Nelson based many of the visual cues in *The Black Art Barbecue* on an engraving by Albrecht Dürer, *St Jerome in his Study* (1514), a work in which each item heaves with symbolism.[1] Indeed, many of the objects in St Jerome's study are given equivalents here. The most traditional *vanitas* emblems – a human skull, an hourglass – are replaced in Nelson's work by a clown mask and an office wall clock. Other objects blend together the macabre, surreal and comedic, combinations common in Nelson's installations. A pumpkin wears a trucker's cap and a rubber Walt Disney 'Goofy' nose, a plastic pig snout sits among tiny toy gremlins.

Books littered around the work station include several copies of *National Geographic*, Heidegger's *Metaphysics* (1953) and *The Rise and Fall of the Third Reich* by William L. Shirer (1960). Like the Dürer engraving, Edgar Allan Poe's *The Fall of the House of Usher* (1839), also here, is noteworthy, owing to the symbolic totalitarian weight given to every object in the crumbling, sickened house in Poe's tale – a weight of objects mirrored here. One can speculate for ever, interpreting Nelson's myriad of historical, literary and artistic sources, lost in a labyrinth worthy of Borges. As the artist has said, 'For me, my work is more like a book than a stage set. The whole point of both is to draw people into a realm, to encourage them to think of what's going on as real.'[2]

What begins to feel most palpably real in *The Black Art Barbecue* is creeping dread. Dürer scholar Karl-Adolf Knappe wrote of *St Jerome* that 'the light streaming in through the window panes, weaving in and out through the picture, becomes a symbol of supernatural light.'[3] In Nelson's room, however, supernatural light emanates from an altogether darker source. The installation is dingy and dim – a single light emanating from underneath the desk. However, you might just notice a shadow thrown on the wall beneath the desk: a large insect, hiding in the dark below, waiting. LMF

1. *St Jerome in his Study* is one of three *Meisterstiche* (master engravings) made by Dürer in 1513 and 1514. The other two prints are *Knight, Death and the Devil* and *Melancholia*.

2. Nelson quoted in the catalogue for São Paulo Bienal 26 (2004).

3. Karl-Adolf Knappe, *Dürer* (New York: Harry N. Abrams, 1964–65).

Purchased March 2000 from
Anthony Reynolds for £20,000
16 mm DVD transfer,
6 mins. 19 secs., 13 frames
P7278

[**2001**] Poland Kraków, Bunkier Sztuki
[**2009**] Israel Tel Aviv Museum of Art

STEVE McQueen's film *Prey* is a rhythmic, deeply poetic work, elusive, yet compelling to watch. The very act of eluding and evading,
however, is a device central to the film, playing, as the title indi-
cates, with concepts of capture and escape. The film begins with a close-
up of a reel-to-reel tape recorder with two large spools, one red and one
green, lying in long summery grass. A sound recording of tap-dancing
is playing from the reels, but the clicking, almost popping, noise could
be anything from an unearthly Morse code to the sonar echo of a bat or
perhaps an arhythmic drumbeat. For roughly the first half of this six-
minute film, we closely watch the tape recorder's reels spin around – a
smooth motion, which, together with the tippity-tap recording, is both
a visualisation of the sound and an incongruous contrast. Suddenly,
the tape recorder appears to move, independently, retreating from the
viewer. As the camera follows, the recorder bumbles along the uneven
grass for a few seconds before taking off, at which point we realise that
it is attached to a small weather balloon. The recorder, with the noise
that it carries, retreats off into the bright white sky, slowly disappear-
ing – audibly and visibly – for the last half of the film. At the end, when
it has all but disappeared, the tape recorder begins to parachute back to
earth, and the camera's angle drops to grass-level once more. The cycle
begins again as the film restarts.

Included in the artist's 1999 Turner Prize exhibition, to some extent
the film is a foray into rich primary colour: red from one tape reel,
green from the other reel, the surrounding grass and a bluish-green
plastic bag that lies nearby. The flight from the viewer halfway through
the film also involves a flight from these rich colours; the object flies
away into a white sky tinged with baby blue, and, one might argue, into
an almost painterly abstraction.

The film is projected large, and at some height above the viewer, so
that one must gaze upwards as the tape recorder rises into the sky. As
the artist has said, 'I want to put people into a situation where they're
sensitive to themselves watching the piece.'[1] In this case, the physicality of the film, together with the almost sculptural qualities of distance
– near and far – created by the sound, exacerbates a sense in the viewer
that is almost akin to a desire: we want the object to return to us.

This desire forms part of a series of subtle decisions by McQueen that
puts the viewer in the position of unsuccessful hunter. Whilst the film
bears some similarity to wildlife documentaries – the unsteady camera
crouched in the grass, observing its strange quarry – the sound of the
tap dancer seems to suggest that an attempt has been made to 'trap' the
dancer within the recording. The tape recorder itself is of a type used
by the CIA and FBI: a further indicator of blunt machines of authority (and one can include the film camera as one of these) attempting to
pin down the essence of a flighty, joyous activity like dance – the swift,
flying feet of Fred Astaire and Ginger Rogers perhaps, which never
touch the ground. The abstract sound might have been captured by the
recorder, but as the sound of foot hitting floor flies away into the sky, it
is almost as though the dancers' feet mock this earthly attempt to strap
them down.   LMF

1. 'Let's get physical', McQueen
interviewed by Patricia Bickers, *Art
Monthly* (December 1996 – January 1997).

Purchased October 1999
from Sadie Coles HQ for £6,168
Iris print on watercolour paper,
each 80 × 60cm
P7238–P7249

[2001] Taiwan Taipei Fine Arts Museum
/ Italy Rome, British Council [2003]
Hungary Budapest, Műcsarnok / Vietnam
Hanoi, British Council [2005] Canada
Vancouver Art Gallery / Canada Ottawa
Art Gallery [2006] Canada Ontario,
Oakville Galleries / Canada Edmonton
Art Gallery / China Guangzhou,
Guangdong Museum of Art [2007] China
Beijing, Capital Museum

I N 1990, the young artist Sarah Lucas, among a notorious group of recent Goldsmiths graduates, embarked on a series of unswervingly confrontational photographic self portraits. The first was 'Eating a Banana' (1990), which was shot in black and white and shows the artist glowering at the camera from behind a floppy dark fringe. For the subsequent images, Lucas photographed herself as a truculent subject, dressed in androgynous garb (heavy boots and knackered jeans) and adopting loutish poses. A fag dangles from her lips, she splays her legs. She adds props laden with innuendo: fried eggs, a toilet, knickers and a fish. Lucas had been keen on the work of feminist theorist Andrea Dworkin while at Goldsmiths College, and cited her as an inspiration, particularly Dworkin's controversial books *Pornography* (1979) and *Intercourse* (1987). Yet it was still something of an epiphany for Lucas when she saw 'Eating a Banana'. She explained that it was the first time she realised that her masculine appearance – which she had until then perceived as a disadvantage – could be used in her art to interrogate gender stereotypes.

Lucas's self portraits, made between 1990 and 1999, chart her career's trajectory. In 1993, she rented a shop with Tracey Emin, selling paraphernalia; this was the setting for 'Self Portrait with Mug of Tea' (1993). Shot from below, her clumpy boots and blue jeans dominate the image, while in her hands she holds a mug and a cigarette. It is the archetypal image of a blue-collar worker on a tea break. Food is a recurrent feature in Lucas's portraits, used as a substitute for body parts. In 'Self Portrait with Fried Eggs' (1996), she is seated on a chair, her breasts covered by two fried eggs. In 'Got a Salmon On' (1997), the artist stands outside a public toilet resting a large fish on her shoulder. Hanging down to her hip, it is a pun on the concept of the female erection. All of the self portraits contest the objectification of the female body, many making direct reference to pornography; in particular, 'Eating a Banana', and 'Summer' (1998), where Lucas is photographed wincing as beer froth is sprayed into her face, approximating an ejaculation. One of her last self portraits, 'Selfish in Bed' (2000),[1] is also one of her funniest and most defiant. Made in the Clerkenwell studio she shared with her then boyfriend Angus Fairhurst, she stands with hands thrust into pockets, daring the viewer to confront gender preconceptions; at her feet a grinning statue of a garden gnome gives the thumbs up.   JL

1. British Council Collection.

Purchased May 2005
from Corvi-Mora for £2,500
Steel, thistles, copper sulphate,
Velcro, 114 × 66 × 51cm
P7568

[2002] Chile Santiago, Museo Nacional
de Bellas Artes [2003] Venezuela
Caracas, Museo Alejandro Otero / Mexico
Mexico City, Museo de Arte Carrillo Gil
/ Colombia Bogotá, Biblioteca Luis-
Angel Arango [2004] Panama Panama
City, Museo de Arte Contemporáneo /
Guatemala Guatemala City, Museo de
Arte Moderna / Brazil São Paulo, SESI
/ Brazil Rio de Janeiro, Museu de Arte
Contemporânea de Niterói [2005]
England Gateshead, Baltic [2006]
England Manchester, various venues /
England Nottingham, various venues /
England Bristol, various venues [2007]
England Ludlow, Meadow Gallery at
Hanbury Hall

ROGER Hiorns is surely, by definition, an alchemist, creating the majority of his sculptural works by placing elements together and letting them fizz, bubble and grow. In *Discipline*, he has dipped thistles in copper sulphate solution, a favourite chemical for this artist, so that gloriously bright blue crystals have bloomed on their surface. Bunches of this precious quarry of weeds have been hung upside down, and fixed with Velcro to several steel rods which are leant against a wall.

These glitteringly bright objects provoke in us a magpie-like attraction, and a desire to run our fingers across a familiar form, feeling how it has become strange. There is always, when looking at Hiorns' sculptures with copper sulphate, an imagining of this process of change – the chemical dip, followed by the slow blossoming of alien crystalline forms on the surface, nurtured by the artist. Contained within these objects is the curiously appealing narrative of their transformation. One only need think of religious tales from any faith, or of comic-book superheroes who begin to transform after drinking a potion or being bitten by a magical animal, to remember just how central transformation narratives are within a culture.

Basic magic is at play here, too. There's no denying the cerulean beauty of the crystal sprouting process, which has for so long delighted children with chemistry sets. My dad bought me a 'grow your own crystals' kit as a child, and I loved it, perhaps primarily because *I* had grown them. The personal satisfaction in overseeing the process might not be lost on Hiorns. Arguably, by covering objects in crystal, he claims them for himself, taking ownership by somehow stilling them, and stopping their progress. One might consider that he has employed the same copper sulphate process on car engines. In *The Birth of the Architect* (2003),[1] for example, a BMW 8-series engine has been scuppered and becomes choked up with a blight of blue gems – creating a functionless bauble of precision engineering.

The power of crystals to generate so visibly relates to a primal property of unstoppable growth within Hiorns' work with materials such as copper sulphate and foam. The importance of propagation in works like *Discipline* might be illuminated (a choice of word which overcooks the point slightly) by Hiorns' later works involving semen on light bulbs (several 'Untitled' works, 2007), a pure marker of territory and DNA, but also of life and growth potential – a force, surely, at the core of human existence.

This is further complicated by the ambiguous 'discipline' of this work's title. Hiorns' sculptures are certainly not objects of abstinence. Against steel rods, thistles and growing crystals look positively excessive: bejewelled, fecund, disobedient things. 'Discipline' also, however, brings other concepts to the table. In Hiorns' work of this period, there is an emphasis on weight, balance and stress, and here there is certainly an equilibrium between the materials and a sense of even weight distribution. The rods lean against a supporting wall, carrying the weight of their heavy bounty with ease. It is the painterly 'discipline' of still life, however, which arguably carries the most weight here. Whilst central to the sculpture, the thistles remain curiously absent, a fugitive presence that one knows is there, but cannot really see. For just as the painter of flowers makes his mark all over them, Hiorns has taken ownership of these weeds in a different way. Claiming them for his own, he presents back to the viewer a life totally stilled – an embalmed bunch of dead, delicious matter. LMF

1. Corvi-Mora, London.

Purchased March 2002
from the artist for £8,000
Pen and ink on paper, 99 × 144cm
P7539

[2002] Brazil São Paulo Bienal [2003]
Canada Vancouver Art Gallery [2004]
Israel Tel Aviv, British Council

A WHISPER into the third millennium and under Michael Landy's instigation, apocalyptic anxieties were played out on Oxford Street. Through the empty display windows of the former C&A department store, shoppers observed an eleven-strong team in blue overalls systematically destroy everything Landy owned over the course of two weeks (10–24 February 2001). All 7,227 items were labelled and catalogued on a database, then passed down 100 metres of conveyor belt to be reduced to their basic materials on a disassembly line. They were finally crushed or granulated, ashes to ashes, dust to dust, generating 5.75 tonnes of material for landfill in direct proportion to the sprawling questions around consumerism, sustainability and personal identity. Moreover, as a performance, *Break Down* became about shared experience, attracting 45,000 visitors and outbursts of concern, moral outrage, hero-worship. 'I liked the idea that the things that were in people's carrier bags were the same things that were travelling round in the yellow plastic trays on the conveyor belts to be destroyed.'[1] Attuned to *Big Brother* and 24-hour news, consumers were receptive to another public breakdown. 'I was scared,' Landy admits. 'That's what pushes me on.'[2]

Like a phoenix from the ashes, this drawing was part of the process of recapitulating an experience that left Landy with nothing. It amounts to an existential anti-shopping list. 'Having nothing was a kind of regression, so I was interested in going back to being a child, to just having a drawing pencil and paper.'[3] Retrospectively, he traces the stages of the disassembly process in pen and ink, employing a line-by-line precision with the pedantry of a military re-enactment. He anatomises his life in terms of the humdrum, a vision of wheelie bins, goggles, odd socks and camera crews, scrutinising the idea that 'somehow at some point we begin to create our own biographies from the things we own or possess.'[4] It is a titanic drawing of minuscule detail, approaching not just a factory floor plan, but medieval cartoons of the Last Judgement categorising the mansions of the righteous and the chambers of the damned (Landy's version is totally devoid of salvation).

Among the legendary Goldsmiths generation of the late 1980s, Landy has emerged as the ultimate Recession artist. His works are few and far between but slice incrementally into the nation's socio-economic crust. 'Worth and value are all wrapped up in what I do.'[5] Following 'Freeze' in 1988 (curated by Damien Hirst, who was in the year below Landy at Goldsmiths) Landy spread his wings in the profusion of disused spaces which pervaded slump-bound London. The C&A's 'closing down!' posters and disembodied check-out signs lingering above the *Break Down* conveyor belts came as a ghostly echo of Landy's earlier end-of-the-world scenario, 'Closing Down Sale' (1992). The Karsten Schubert gallery had been turned into an apocalyptic bargain basement, full of trolleys of oddments from skips and day-glo starbursts – 'Meltdown Madness Sale!' 'Everything Must Go!' 'Last Day!' – under a voiceover urging visitors to buy ('crazy! crazy! crazy!') in tones of spiralling hysteria. (Nothing sold and it all ended up in landfill via *Break Down*.)

A forefather to Landy's modes of destruction is Jean Tinguely – Landy remembers visiting the Tinguely retrospective (Tate Gallery, 1982) then a textiles student at Loughborough College of Art, and being deeply impressed. Both are nuts and bolts artists, exploring the relativity of component parts. Most conspicuously, the present drawing has Tinguely's enormous *Méta-matic 17* (1959)[6] in the background, a car-like machine made out of scrap materials that produced 40,000 drawings by means of a balloon filled with exhaust gas. Landy's intricate drawing ricochets off Tinguely's automatic scribbles. Carefully worked, and inscribed with his personal style and signature, it is a precious, poignant item and a sly postscript to the cataclysm of the *Break Down* performance.   DF

1. Landy in conversation with James Lingwood, in *Michael Landy: Everything Must Go!* (London: Ridinghouse, 2008), 106.

2. Landy, in conversation at the Prince's Drawing School (January 2009).

3. Landy (2008), 109.

4. Ibid., 107.

5. Landy, Prince's Drawing School (2009).

6. Moderna Museet, Stockholm.

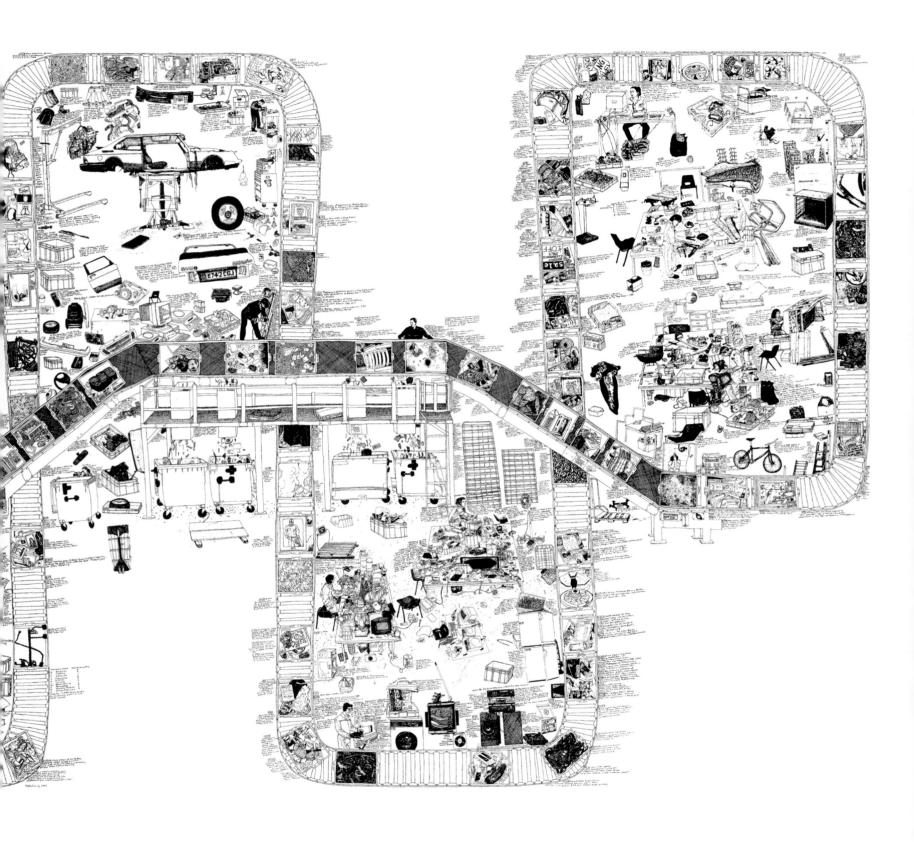

Martin Boyce
Mobile (Being with you is like the new past), 2002

Purchased August 2002 from
The Modern Institute for £8,000
Painted steel, chain, wire, altered
Jacobsen 3107 chairs, dimensions
variable

P7667

[2002] Chile Santiago, Museo Nacional
de Bellas Artes [2003] Venezuela
Caracas, Museo Alejandro Otero /
Mexico Mexico City, Museo Carrillo Gil
/ Colombia Bogotá, Biblioteca Luis-
Angel Arango [2004] Panama Panama
City, Museo de Arte Contemporáneo /
Guatemala Guatemala City, Museo de
Arte Moderna / Brazil São Paulo, SESI
/ Brazil Rio de Janeiro, Museu de Arte
Contemporânea de Niterói [2005] Oman
Muscat, British Council

GHOSTS are ever present in the work of Martin Boyce, and *Mobile (Being with you is like the new past)* is no exception. At first glance, what appear to be oddly formless, dark shapes hang from a mobile, floating in the air like unlikely spirits, with a mixture of grace and awkwardness. The structure of the work suggests a more ominous rendering of the mobiles of Alexander Calder, who invented the modern mobile in 1931. Suspended in Boyce's sculpture, however, are not the distinctly abstract shapes of which Calder was fond, but parts of chairs designed by the Danish architect and designer Arne Jacobsen. The parts come from the *3107 Chair*, designed in 1955, also known as the 'series 7' chair, perhaps the design for which Jacobsen is best known.

As in much of Boyce's work from this period, there is a fascination with icons of Modernist design and architecture, and with the continuing atmospheres and ideologies that might be contained within the remaining objects. As well as Jacobsen, the designers Charles and Ray Eames play an important role for Boyce at this time. The ghostly feel of this series of works, often grouped together in atmospheric environments, might be encapsulated by the phrase 'undead dreams', which can be read on the artist's sculptures of ventilation grills. *Phantom Limb (Undead Dreams)* (2003),[1] a contemporaneous work, is a sculpture based on an Eames' 'Splint Sculpture' (1942), which reappears in Boyce's work, altered, and resembling a cartoon phantom.

What is, to some extent, at stake here is the idea of built-in obsolescence that was becoming common in American manufacturing in the mid 20th century, with a burgeoning economy supported by a willingness to discard objects. The dreams for Modernist design, particularly seen in California during this period, were based in utopian solutions for a post-war economy: usable objects that might change the way the average family lived. Ultimately, however, over time these 'classic' pieces of design became luxury commodities for the rich and educated. In *Mobile*, the principles of democratic design and 'form follows function' are ridiculed, as the chairs' seats and backs dangle out of reach, impossible to use. Boyce's reframing of these design 'icons' speculates that Modernism itself also contained built-in obsolescence from the start. Approaching these 50-year-old ghosts now, as Will Bradley has commented, reveals the 'emotional bond' of Modernism – not only in relation to ideas, but in 'the acceptance that certain formal strategies could usefully represent those ideas. That acceptance has gone. Few people, now, would be fooled into thinking that pretty flowers or even thoughtful design could bridge the gaping holes in our social and political structures.'[2]

And, yet. What if? What utopian hope remains in these chairs, these designs, untapped? Is another, alternative future or present discernible? The subtitle of Boyce's mobile, *Being with you is like the new past*, hints at the work's peculiar relationship to time. 'Being with' someone connotes the present, or at least presentness, but the invocation of a past that is 'new' loosens its temporality. Boyce has spoken of his work with Eames' sculptures as creating 'derailed' versions of the original – objects that might have ended up in the present via a parallel route. Whether these objects come from a time that is better or worse is hard to say. However, as rendered by Boyce, they are charged with different, fluctuating potentials. They hover, above the ground, in a kind of limbo, a spectral waiting area for other imagined futures.   LMF

1. First shown at RomaRomaRoma, Rome, in 'Undead Dreams' (2003).

2. Will Bradley, 'California ghosts and flowers', in *Martin Boyce: Undead Dreams* (London: Koenig, 2003), 12.

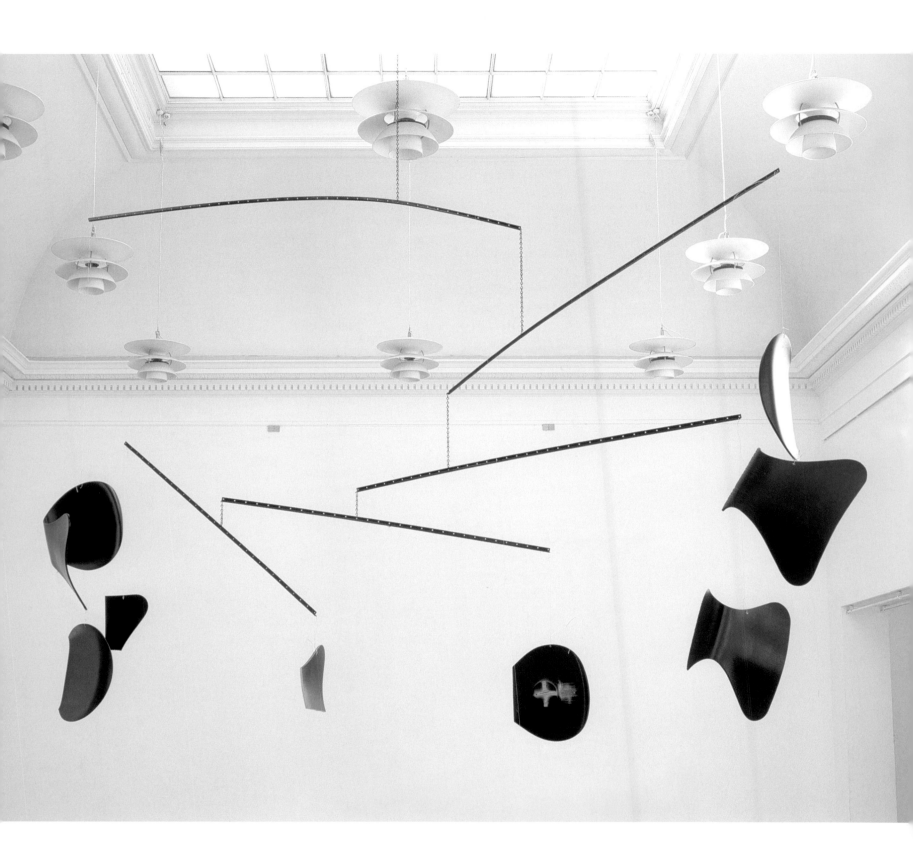

Purchased April 2004 from
Lehmann Maupin for $22,500
500 red gerbera, glass and fittings,
247 × 130.8 × 2.5cm
P7871

[2007] England London, British Council

LIKE an impossible fairytale task from Rumpelstiltskin – who ordered the miller's daughter to spin straw into gold – all attempts to preserve beauty must fail. Anya Gallaccio's *Preserve Beauty*, however, valiantly takes up the challenge. Five hundred red gerberas are pressed between a sheet of glass and the wall, in a rough grid formation. Pretty maids all in a row. In time, the flowers begin to decompose, assisted by the glass press. Withering and shrivelling, they fall out of place, or to the floor, slowly rotting. What begins bonny and blithe, turns dull and crackled, and covered with a fluffy grey mould.

In a previous incarnation in 1991, *Preserve Beauty* was installed in the window of Karsten Schubert gallery in London, so that the flowers faced out to the people passing in the street. Inside the gallery, the green stalks seemed to 'face' away from the viewer, which highlighted the anthropomorphic quality of the gerberas – showing off and jostling for attention. Their fading dying 'faces', both in reality and in the memories of those who saw them in the window, align the work with *Tense II* (1991),[1] from the same year, in which the artist placed a group of unfixed photographs under a skylight so that the faces gradually faded from view.

Gerberas are unequivocally cheery flowers – Gallaccio's mass-produced pop readymade. Their bright, daisy shape is the kind that a child would draw if asked to draw a flower. As with the Duchampian readymade, there is no privileging of the artist's relationship with the material – no brush strokes or fingerprints. The process-based aspects of the work are completed by a combination of time and a site's natural atmospheric conditions, including light, heat, moisture and bacteria. Another, related, privilege also denied, however, is our ability to 'see' the work. As Ralph Rugoff explains,

Gallaccio's mutable flower pieces defy any illusion that we, as spectators, are privy to a transcendent or authentic experience – there is no true moment, no definitive point of view, for our encounter with this art, as the work we witness today will have changed in a week's time, and ultimately remains as elusive and changeable as that mysterious entity, the self.[2]

Discrete experiences of beauty and art are pinpricks in large acres of time. Flowers are slowly grown, and then, in one quick moment, cut – and at their very prime. The 'unbearable' nature of beauty, as described by Albert Camus, is the offer of 'for a minute the glimpse of an eternity that we should like to stretch out over the whole of time'.[3] *Preserve Beauty* may thus be read as a knowingly futile attempt, searching for beauty in the long process, rather than the fleeting moment.

However, whilst Gallaccio's sculptural installations might seem celebratory, there is an implicit violence in her work, related to the 500 tiny deaths that we see before us. This relationship might be read through the colours red and green, complementary colours that have figured in several of Gallaccio's most important works. *Red on Green*, for example, exhibited at the ICA in 1992, consisted of the red heads of 10,000 tea roses placed on a bed of green stalks and thorns.[4] Over time, the fat floating blooms shrunk and died, to reveal the sharp thorns beneath. The connotations of the two colours are well known – red with passion, death, and blood spilled, and green with new life of nature: both beautiful, both violent. It is, to borrow the title of a woodland scene by Gallaccio, *the way things are – green with red* (2000).[5]

LMF

1. Shown at the Museum of Installation, Site Three, Surrey Docks, London (1991).

2. Ralph Rugoff, *Anya Gallaccio: Chasing Rainbows* (Glasgow / Newcastle-upon-Tyne: Tramway / Locus+, 1999), 12.

3. Albert Camus, *Notebooks 1935–1951* (London: Marlowe, 1998), 6.

4. *Red on Green* was last shown at Tate, in 'The Art of the Garden' (2004). Private collection.

5. Lehmann Maupin, New York. Edition of 5.

Purchased March 2007
from the artists for £25,000
Mixed media, dimensions variable
P8028

[2007] Serbia Belgrade, Museum of
Contemporary Art [2008] France Paris,
Palais de Tokyo

J EREMY Deller and Alan Kane know that they tread a delicate
line with the *Folk Archive*. Their collection and documentation of
contemporary popular art in the UK at the turn of the century
is situated in the rich seam between art and anthropology – and
the artists knew they ran the risk of exploiting their subjects. As they
conceded from the start, 'For those interested in an anthropological
approach, we must apologise for the rather too knowing misuse of the
phrase "archive" and an artistic casualness with details. For all involved
in the folk or vernacular cultural scenes we must similarly apologise for
the cheap "folk" shot and a fly-by-night plundering of whole worlds.'[1] It
is only through these two small betrayals, however, that we are able to
see what Deller and Kane are getting at with *Folk Archive*, and that is: a
large public heart beating out creativity under the radar of a sanctified
art world.

The archive contains relics from festivals and celebrations across
Britain, ancient and modern, as well as the ignored efforts of owners of
cafes, burger vans and shops, and the somewhat more politicised efforts
from protesters and prison inmates. Each work is made by people who
have, quite simply, created things to convey their message, be it love,
sadness, rage, or a nice cup of tea. The beautifully hand-embroidered
male wrestling costumes of Cumberland and Westmoreland, for
example, with their curling images of dainty flowers and leaves, are
often picked out by commentators as vernacular and culturally specific.
The decorative costumes are worn by men taking part in wrestling
matches as part of the Egremont Crab Fair in Cumbria, a festival
established in 1387 and encompassing a bewildering array of parades
and contests. As Tom Morton describes, 'This D. H. Lawrence-like
reframing of masculinity as something intertwined with the fecund stuff
of stamens and petals wouldn't play on a national stage (no TV hard
man would be seen dead in rose-patterned briefs), but in this small
community of wrestling enthusiasts it seems to make sense.'[2]

As well as long-held (and often rural) traditions, however, proper pop
is present too. Memorials to Princess Diana are included, as is a painting of 'The Simpsons' on a Sheffield wall, albeit bearing little resemblance to the familiar cartoon characters. Viewers might also stumble
across a pincushion made in the shape of a St John's Ambulance vehicle,
a watercolour pencil drawing of a topless Page 3 stunner pulling a pint,
flower arrangements, customised motorcycling helmets and birthday
messages.

Not once, however, will you find an underhand sneer or snigger
from the artists who collected and presented this work. Arguably, what
underpins *Folk Archive* is an understanding that 'it is popular culture
now, not religion, that is the heart of a heartless world.'[3] The acts of love
here range from the grand to the quotidian, impossible to view with
the cool eye of contemporary art. As Deller comments, 'Warhol said
that pop art was about liking things, whereas for me folk art is about
loving things.'[4] Though there are political banners and artworks here,
perhaps the most politicised thing about *Folk Archive* is that it reveals a
basic, institutionalised mistrust of the general public, which is, in turn,
revealed to be unfounded. It is possible to discern here a general public
that is not a passive, shuffling and pedestrian herd, but a mobilised set
of individuals who create, make, change and organise. Deller and Kane,
whilst openly betraying their subjects, reveal a potentially revolutionary,
yet heartfelt, force that was there all along. LMF

1. Jeremy Deller and Alan Kane, *Folk
Archive: Contemporary Popular Art from
the* UK (London: Book Works, 2005), 2.

2. Tom Morton, 'Folk Archive', *Frieze*, 93
(September 2005), 134.

3. David Beech, 'High on Good Shit:
Towards an ethical relation to popular
culture', in Jeremy Deller, *Life is to Blame
for Everything: Collected work & projects
1992–99* (London: Salon 3, 2001), 94.

4. Deller quoted by Tania Branigan,
'Profile', *The Guardian* (3 December
2004), 13.

Exhibition Histories

This section provides titles and dates for the exhibitions in which individual catalogue works have been included. Entries are ordered alphabetically by artist.

Frank Auerbach b.1931

20 | *The Camden Theatre* 1976

1984 Home and Abroad: An Exhibition of Recent Acquisitions for the Arts Council and the British Council Collections
1984–85 The Proper Study
1987–88 British Figurative Painting: A Matter of Paint

Martin Boyce b.1967

43 | *Mobile (Being with you is like the new past)* 2002

2002–04 Still Life

Patrick Caulfield 1936–2005

14 | *View Inside a Cave* 1965

1968 Junge Generation Großbritannien
1969 Marks on a Canvas
1970 British Painting and Sculpture 1960–1970
1972 British Paintings 1945–1970
1978 Biennale de Paris '59–'73
1990–91 For a Wider World

Tony Cragg b.1949

26 | *Canoe* 1982

1983 Tema Celeste
1983–84 São Paulo Bienal 17
1990–91 For a Wider World
1992 New Voices
1994–96 A Changing World: 50 Years of Sculpture from the British Council Collection
1996 Voyages sans passeport
1997–2000 A Changed World
1999 Le Musée à l'heure anglaise
2001 Field Day: Sculpture from Britain
2007 Il Settimo Splendore: La modernità della malinconia

Michael Craig-Martin b.1941

Picturing: iron, watch, safety pin, pliers 1978

1982 5th Indian Triennale
1986 Between Object and Image: Contemporary British Sculpture
1994–96 A Changing World: 50 Years of Sculpture from the British Council Collection
1997–2000 A Changed World
1997–2001 Drawing Distinctions (drawing)
2001 Field Day: Sculpture from Britain
2004 From Moore to Hirst: Sixty Years of British Sculpture
2008 Long Distance Information

Richard Deacon b.1949

25 | *Boys and Girls (come out to play)* 1982

1983 Richard Deacon
1983–84 São Paulo Bienal 17
1984 Turner Prize
1984 Richard Deacon: Sculpture
1985 49th Carnegie International Exhibition
1987–88 The Analytical Theatre – Contemporary Brit Art
1989 British Sculpture 1960–1988
1989 Richard Deacon
1990–91 For a Wider World
1992 New Voices
1994–96 A Changing World: 50 Years of Sculpture from the British Council Collection
1996 Un Siècle de sculpture anglaise
1996 Voyages sans passeport
1997–2000 A Changed World
2001 Field Day: Sculpture from Britain
2002–03 Blast to Freeze: British Art in the 20th Century
2004 Turning Points: 20th Century British Sculpture
2004 From Moore to Hirst: Sixty Years of British Sculpture
2005 Henry Moore: Epoch and Echo, English Sculpture in the 20th Century

Peter Doig b.1959

31 | *Hill Houses* 1990–91

1992–97 New Voices
2000–02 Landscape

Angus Fairhurst 1966–2008

36 | *A Cheap and Ill-Fitting Gorilla Suit* 1995

1997–99 Dimensions Variable

Lucian Freud b.1922

8 | *Girl with Roses* 1947–48

1949 Contemporary British Art from the Collections of the Arts Council and the British Council
1950 Contemporary British Painting and Sculpture 1925–1950
1951 British Painting 1925–1950: First Anthology
1951 São Paulo Bienal 1
1952 Slade School Exhibition
1951 Recent Trends in Realist Painting
1954 XXVII Venice Biennale
1955 Young British Painters
1956 British Art 1900–1955
1957 64th Spring Exhibition
1958 Lucian Freud
1960 British Painting 1720–1960
1963–64 Contemporary British Painting 1900–1962
1972 British Paintings 1945–1970
1972–73 Decade 40's
1975 British Portraits
1976–77 Six Paintings from the British Council Collection

1978 20th Century Portraits
1980 Jubilee Exhibition
1982 XL Venice Biennale, International Exhibition
1984 Home and Abroad: An Exhibition of Recent Acquisitions for the Arts Council and the British Council Collections
1984–85 The Proper Study
1986 Artist and Model
1987 British Art in the 20th Century
1987–88 Lucian Freud: Paintings
1988 Lucian Freud
1951 100 Years of Art in Britain
1988–89 Centenary Exhibition – 100 Years of British Art
1990–91 For a Wider World
1992–93 Lucian Freud: Paintings and Works on Paper 1940–1991
1993–94 Lucian Freud: Recent Work
1994 Réalités noires
1995–96 From London
1996 Lucian Freud: Paintings and Etchings
1998 L'École de Londres: de Bacon à Bevan
2001 Travelling Companions: Chardin and Freud
2002–03 Lucian Freud
2005 Lucian Freud
2007 The Mirror and the Mask: The Portrait in the Age of Picasso British Vision: Observation and Imagination in British Art 1750–1950
2008 Lucian Freud

Gilbert & George b.1943 and 1942

24 | *Intellectual Depression* 1980

1982 Aspects of British Art Today
1984–85 Gilbert and George
1987 Current Affairs: British Painting and Sculpture in the 1980s
1990–91 For a Wider World
1997 Gilbert and George
1997–2000 A Changed World
1999 Le Musée à l'heure anglaise

Douglas Gordon b.1966

34 | *10 ms⁻¹* 1994

1995 General Release: Young British Artists
1995–96 British Art Show 4
1996 Hide and Seek
1997 Treasure Island
1997–99 Dimensions Variable
2000 A Changed World
2001 Field Day: Sculpture from Britain
2001 Loop – Alles auf Anfang
2001 Black Box Recorder
2002 The Big Video Screening
2004 From Moore to Hirst: Sixty Years of British Sculpture
2006 Monologue / Dialogue
2006–07 Aftershock: Contemporary British Art 1990–2006

Antony Gormley b.1950

29 | *Out of this World* 1983–84

1997–2000 A Changed World
1999 Le Musée à l'heure anglaise
2001 Field Day: Sculpture from Britain
2002 About Face: Get Your Head Around Sculpture
2004 From Moore to Hirst: Sixty Years of British Sculpture

Richard Hamilton b.1922

16 | *The Solomon R. Guggenheim (White), (Black), (Chromium)* 1970

1974–87 Figuration and Fantasy: Contemporary British Prints
2003–07 As Is When: A Boom in British Printmaking 1961–1972
2008 Revolutions 1968

Mona Hatoum b.1952

37 | *Prayer Mat* 1995

1995 4th International Istanbul Biennial
1997–99 Dimensions Variable
2004 From Moore to Hirst: Sixty Years of British Sculpture
2006 Without Boundaries: Seventeen Ways of Looking
2008 Long Distance Information

Tim Head b.1946

22 | *Still Life* 1978

1979 Uncertain art anglais: Selection d'artistes britanniques 1970–1979
1979 JP2: Art actuel en Belgique et en Grande-Bretagne
1980 British Art Now: An American Perspective
1981 Il Deserto
1994–96 A Changing World: 50 Years of Sculpture from the British Council Collection
1996 Voyages sans passeport
1998–2000 A Changed World

Barbara Hepworth 1903–75

9 | *Rhythmic Form* 1949

1950 XXV Venice Biennale
1950 Barbara Hepworth: New Sculpture and Drawings
1951 Abstract Artists of Three Nations
1951 Barbara Hepworth
1954 Barbara Hepworth: Retrospective Exhibition of Carvings and Drawings 1927–1954
1956 British Art 1900–1955
1959–60 São Paulo Bienal 5
1964–66 Barbara Hepworth Retrospective 1935–64
1968 Barbara Hepworth
1970 Barbara Hepworth
1972–73 Decade 40's
1976 Kunst in Europa 1920–1960

1981 British Sculpture in the Twentieth Century: Part 1, Image and Form 1910–1950
1987 L'Art en Europe 1946–53
1994–95 Barbara Hepworth: A Retrospective
1999 Ten for the Century: A View of Sculpture in Britain
2002 Pre-Columbian and 20th Century Art
2003 Barbara Hepworth Centenary Exhibition
2004 Turning Points: 20th Century British Sculpture
2004 From Moore to Hirst: Sixty Years of British Sculpture
2006 Barbara Hepworth

Roger Hiorns b.1975

41 | *Discipline* 2002

2002–04 Still Life
2005–06 British Art Show 6
2007 Still Life

Damien Hirst b.1965

33 | *Apotryptophanae* 1994

1997–99 Dimensions Variable
2001 Field Day: Sculpture from Britain
2008 History in the Making: A Retrospective of the Turner Prize

David Hockney b.1937

12 | *Man in a Museum (or You are in the Wrong Movie)* 1962

1970 David Hockney: Painting, Prints and Drawings 1960–1970
1972 British Paintings 1945–1970
1976 Arte inglese oggi 1960–76
1977 La Peinture britannique de Gainsborough à Bacon
1983–85 Hockney Paints the Stage
1984 El Gran Teatro de David Hockney
1988–89 David Hockney: A Retrospective
1989 David Hockney
1990–91 For a Wider World
1992 Life into Paint
2001 David Hockney: Painting 1960–2000
2005 Metamorphosis: British Arts of the Sixties
2006 David Hockney: New Ways of Seeing
2006 David Hockney – From Bradford to Hollywood and Back Again
2008 A Guest of Honour: From Francis Bacon to Peter Doig

Howard Hodgkin b.1932

21 | *Still Life in a Restaurant* 1976–79

1981 Howard Hodgkin
1982–83 13 Britische Künstler: Eine Ausstellung über Malerei
1984–85 XLI Venice Biennale
1987 Current Affairs: British Painting and Sculpture in the 1980s
1988 100 Years of Art in Britain

1990–91 For a Wider World
1995–96 Howard Hodgkin: Paintings
2002–03 Blast to Freeze: British
Art in the 20th Century

Alan Kane b.1961
and **Jeremy Deller** b.1966

45 | *The Folk Archive* 2005

2007 Breaking Step: Displacement, Compassion
and Humour in Recent British Art
2008 Jeremy Deller: From One Revolution to Another

Anish Kapoor b.1954

28 | *The Chant of Blue* 1983

1983–84 São Paulo Bienal 17
1990–91 For a Wider World
1992 New Voices
1994–96 A Changing World: 50 Years of
Sculpture from the British Council Collection
1997–2000 A Changed World
2001 Field Day: Sculpture from Britain
2004 Turning Points: 20th Century British Sculpture

Leon Kossoff b.1926

19 | *View of Dalston Junction* 1974

1997 Treasure Island
1998 L'École de Londres: de Bacon à Bevan

Michael Landy b.1963

42 | *Break Down* 2002

2002 São Paulo Bienal 25
2003 For the Record: Drawing Contemporary Life

Peter Lanyon 1918–64

10 | *Bojewyan Farms* 1951–52

1968 Peter Lanyon
1978 Peter Lanyon: Paintings, Drawings
and Constructions 1937–64
1985–89 St Ives 1939–64: Twenty-Five Years
of Painting, Sculpture and Pottery
1987 L'Art en Europe 1946–53
1990–91 For a Wider World
1992–93 Peter Lanyon: Air, Land and Sea
1997–99 The Fifties
2000 Peter Lanyon: Coastal Journey

Richard Long b.1945

23 | *Stone Line* 1979

1990–91 For a Wider World
2005 Making Time
2008 Long Distance Information

Sarah Lucas b.1962

40 | from *Self Portraits 1990–1999* 1999

2001 Field Day: Sculpture from Britain
2003 Micro/Macro
2005–06 Body: New Art from the UK
2006–07 Aftershock: Contemporary
British Art 1990–2006

Steve McQueen b.1969

39 | *Prey* 1999

2001 Black Box Recorder
2009 Sounds and Visions: Artists' Films and
Video from Europe – The Last Decade

Henry Moore 1898–1986

3 | *Girl with Clasped Hands* 1930

1948 XXIV Venice Biennale
1949 Henry Moore: Sculpture and Drawings 1923–1948
1949–51 Henry Moore: Sculpture
and Drawings 1923–1948
1951 Henry Moore Exhibition
1952 The Meaning of Sculpture
1952–53 Henry Moore
1953 São Paulo Bienal 2
1955–59 Henry Moore
1959–60 Henry Moore 1927–1958
1960–61 Henry Moore: Sculpture
and Drawings 1927–1959
1963 Henry Moore: An Exhibition
of Sculpture and Drawings
1964–65 Henry Moore: Esculturas y Dibujos 1928–1962
1966–67 Henry Moore: Sculpture and
Drawings from 1924 to 1964
1966–67 Some Sculptures and
Drawings by Henry Moore?
1969–70 Henry Moore: Exhibition
of Sculpture and Drawings
1972 Henry Moore
1973 Henry Moore: Retrospective (1927–1970)
1977 Henry Moore: Sculptures et dessins
1981–82 Henry Moore: Sculpture,
Drawings and Graphics 1921–1981
1982–83 Henry Moore: Esculturas,
Dibujos, Grabados – Obras 1921–1982
1986 The Art of Henry Moore: Sculptures,
Drawings and Graphics 1921 to 1984
1987 Henry Moore: Sculptures, Drawings
and Graphics 1922 to 1984
1988 Henry Moore
1990–91 For a Wider World
1992 Henry Moore 1898–1986
1993 Henry Moore
1995 Henry Moore: A Retrospective
1995 Henry Moore: Sculture Disigni Incisioni Arazzi
1996 Henry Moore: From the Inside Out
1997 Henry Moore: Hacia el Futuro
1998 Henry Moore: Friendship and Influence
1999 Kunstwelten im Dialog: Von
Gauguin zur globalen Gegenwart
2000–01 Henry Moore in China
2000–01 Le Corps mis a nu: 40 sculptures
de Rodin à Vanessa Beecroft

2002–03 Blast to Freeze: British Art in the 20th Century
2003 Nackt! Female Visions, Painter's Intentions:
The Rise of Modernism
2004 Six European Masters: Redefining the Body
2004 From Moore to Hirst: Sixty
Years of British Sculpture
2005 Henry Moore: Uma Restrospetiva
2006 Henry Moore

4 | *Composition* 1933

1948 XXIV Venice Biennale
1949 Henry Moore: Sculpture and Drawings 1923–1948
1949–51 Henry Moore: Sculpture
and Drawings 1923–1948
1951 Henry Moore Exhibition
1952 The Meaning of Sculpture
1952–53 Henry Moore
1953 Henry Moore: Skulpturer och teckningar
1953 São Paulo Bienal 2
1955–59 Henry Moore: Izložba Skulpture i Crteža
1959–60 Henry Moore 1927–1958
1960–61 Henry Moore: Sculpture
and Drawings 1927–1959
1966–67 Henry Moore: Sculpture and
Drawings from 1924 to 1964
1968–69 Henry Moore
1972 Henry Moore
1973 Henry Moore: Retrospective (1921–1970)
1974 Art Then: Eight English Artists, 1924–40
1977 Henry Moore: Sculptures et dessins
1978 Unit One
1981–82 Henry Moore: Sculpture,
Drawings and Graphics 1921–1981
1982 Henry Moore: Helmet-Head
1982–83 Henry Moore: Early Carvings 1920–1940
1986 The Art of Henry Moore: Sculptures,
Drawings and Graphics 1921 to 1984
1987 Henry Moore: Sculptures, Drawings
and Graphics 1922 to 1984
1990–91 For a Wider World
2004 Henry Moore at Dulwich Picture Gallery
2004 From Moore to Hirst: Sixty
Years of British Sculpture
2006 Henry Moore
2007 Europe, Russia, Europe

5 | *Mother and Child* 1936

1948 XXIV Venice Biennale
1949 Henry Moore: Sculpture and Drawings 1923–1948
1949–51 Henry Moore: Sculpture
and Drawings 1923–1948
1951 Henry Moore Exhibition
1952 The Meaning of Sculpture
1952 Modern Religious Art
1953 São Paulo Bienal 2
1954–59 Henry Moore
1960–61 Henry Moore: Sculpture
and Drawings 1927–1959
1963 Henry Moore: An Exhibition
of Sculpture and Drawings
1964–65 Henry Moore: Esculturas y Dibujos 1928–1962
1966–67 Henry Moore: Sculpture and
Drawings from 1924 To 1964
1967 Some Sculptures and Drawings by Henry Moore
1969–70 Henry Moore: Exhibition
of Sculpture and Drawings
1971 The Human Figure in the Plastic Arts
1972 Henry Moore
1973 Henry Moore: Retrospective (1927–1970)

Paul Nash 1889–1946

1 | *Landscape of the Megaliths* 1934

Mike Nelson b.1967

38 | *The Black Art Barbecue, San Antonio, August 1961* 1998

Ben Nicholson 1894–1982

2 | *1935 (White Relief)* 1935

7 | *11 November 1947 (Mousehole)* 1947

Chris Ofili b.1968

32 | *Painting with Shit on it* 1993

Eduardo Paolozzi 1924–2005

13 | *Diana as an Engine I* 1963–66

Victor Pasmore 1908–98

11 | *Abstract in White, Black, Brown and Lilac* 1957

Bridget Riley b.1931

15 | *Cataract 3* 1967

1999 Bridget Riley: Paintings from the 1960s and 70s
1999 Bridget Riley: Selected Paintings 1961–1999
2000 Bridget Riley: Reconnaissance
2001 Palomino
2002–03 Blast to Freeze: British
Art in the 20th Century
2003 Einbildung: Das Wahrnehmen in der Kunst
2004–05 Bridget Riley: Paintings
and Drawings 1961–2004
2008 Bridget Riley

Sean Scully b.1945

17 | *Red Light* 1972

1973 La Peinture anglaise aujourd'hui
1974 XI Biennale internationale d'art
1990–91 For a Wider World

Graham Sutherland 1903–80

6 | *Thorn Trees* 1945

1946 Exposition internationale de peintures modernes
1947–48 La Jeune Peinture en Grande-Bretagne
1948 Engelsk Nutidskonst
1948–49 Eleven British Artists
1949 Contemporary Art from Great
Britain, United States and France
1950–51 Contemporary Paintings
1952–53 XXVI Venice Biennale
1953 Graham Sutherland
1954 Europa Kunst 1953–1954
1954–55 Graham Sutherland: Drawings and Gouaches
1955 São Paulo Bienal 3
1956 British Art 1900–1955
1957 4th International Exhibition
of Contemporary Art
1958 50 Years of Modern Art
1959 Graham Sutherland
1960 British Painting 1720–1960
1962 Arte britânica no século XX
1963–64 Some Aspects of
Contemporary British Painting
1964 Deux Siècles de peinture britannique 1750–1950
1965–66 Graham Sutherland
1967 Graham Sutherland
1970 Expo 70
1972 IX Biennale internationale d'art
1972–73 Decade 40's
1975–76 British Painting 1900–1960
1976–77 Six Paintings from the
British Council Collection
1980 Jubilee Exhibition
1982 Graham Sutherland
1984 Ruhrfestspiele Recklinghausen
1984 Home and Abroad: An Exhibition of Recent
1984 Acquisitions for the Arts Council
and the British Council Collections
1987 A Paradise Lost: The Neo-Romantic
Imagination in Britain 1935–55
1988 Graham Sutherland
1990–91 For a Wider World
1993 Herbert Read: A British Vision of World Art
1994 Réalités noires
1998 Sutherland: Une Retrospective
2002–03 Blast to Freeze: British
Art in the 20th Century

2005 Graham Sutherland: Landscapes,
War Scenes, Portraits 1924–1950
2007 British Vision: Observation and
Imagination in British Art 1750–1950
2008 From Destruction to Abstraction:
British art in the 1940s and 1950s
2009 Graham Sutherland

Euan Uglow 1932–2000

18 | *Georgia* 1973

1989–90 Picturing People: British
Figurative Art Since 1945
1992 British Figurative Painting of the 20th Century
2000 La Mirada Fuerte: Pintura figurativa de Londres
2003 Spotlight on Euan Uglow
2003 Euan Uglow – Controlled
Passion: Fifty Years of Painting

Mark Wallinger b.1959

35 | *Royal Ascot* 1994

1997–99 Dimensions Variable
2001 Century City: Art and Culture
in the Modern Metropolis
2002 Family
2003 Rituale
2006–07 Aftershock: Contemporary
British Art 1990–2006

Rachel Whiteread b.1963

30 | *False Door* 1990

1991 Metropolis
1992 New Voices
1995 New Art from Britain
1997–2000 A Changed World
1999 Le Musée à l'heure anglaise
2001 Field Day: Sculpture from Britain
2002–03 Blast to Freeze: British Art in the
20th Century
2003 Sculpture in The Close
2003–04 Rachel Whiteread

Bill Woodrow b.1948

27 | *Long Distance Information* 1983

1983 Beaver, Bomb and Fossil
1983–84 São Paulo Bienal 17
1985–86 Space Invaders
1988 Object and Image: Aspects
of British Art in the 1980s
1990–91 For a Wider World
1992 New Voices
1994–96 A Changing World: 50 Years of
Sculpture from the British Council Collection
1997–2000 A Changed World
1999 Le Musée à l'heure anglaise
2001 Object
2008 Long Distance Information

ACKNOWLEDGEMENTS

With thanks to: Chris Aldgate, Marcus Alexander, Matt Arthurs, Sinta Berry, Iwona Blazwick, Silvia Bordin, Tony Connor, Paul Eastman, Sarah Gillett, Julian Hodges, Catherine Jay, Patrick Lears, Tim Marlow, Deborah Prosser, Richard Riley, Shamita Sharmacharja, Richard Shone, Candy Stobbs, Andrea Tarsia, Louise Wright

And to previous members of Visual Arts Department whose stewardship and prescience in recent decades have enriched the Collection: Julian Andrews, Ian Barker, Lewis Biggs, Caroline Douglas, Ann Elliott, Jacqueline Ford, Gerald Forty, Ann Gallagher, Teresa Gleadowe, Joanna Gutteridge, Gill Hedley, Colin Ledwith, Henry Meyric Hughes, Brett Rogers, Muriel Wilson

COLOPHON

Published by British Council
10 Spring Gardens, London SW1A 2BN
on the occasion of the exhibition at
Whitechapel Gallery, London,
5 April to 14 June 2009

© British Council, 2009

ISBN 978 086355 622 7

Head of Collections: Diana Eccles
Exhibition Organiser: Hannah Hunt

Catalogue Research: Janice West
Catalogue edited by Katie Boot, Diana Eccles and Hannah Hunt

Catalogue Photographers: Nina Altman, Prudence Cumming Associates, Serge Hasenböhler, Mike Fear, John Riddy, Rodney Todd-White & Son, Edward Woodman

Designed & typeset in Warnock by Dalrymple
Printed in Belgium by Die Keure

Cover: detail from Roger Hiorns, *Discipline*, 2002 (no.41)

Inside cover: Acquisitions Ledger, British Council Collection, 1930s

Title spread: detail from Ben Nicholson, *1935 (White Relief)*, 1935 (no.2)